Preface

Quick, name a few famous Kentuckians. Some stand out immediately: Daniel Boone, Abraham Lincoln, Mary Todd Lincoln, Colonel Sanders, Muhammad Ali. Upon further reflection, other less obvious luminaries come to mind, such as the emancipationist Cassius M. Clay, Kit Carson, Jefferson Davis, D. W. Griffith, Loretta Lynn, and Floyd Collins.

But there is another classification of those Kentucky natives who, for better or worse, have a place in history. These are people who were once household names, but hardly are remembered now; people who never became famous, but should have. Kentuckians who are peculiar footnotes to history: eccentrics, dreamers, madmen, visionaries, con artists, reformers, criminals. Kentuckians who, in the words of Thoreau, marched to the beat of their own drummers, whatever the consequences. These are the offbeat Kentuckians.

Some of the persons discussed in this book were born in the state and made names for themselves while still residents, i.e. Nathan Stubblefield and John Shell. Some were born in Kentucky but rose to prominence elsewhere, such as Carry Nation and Phil Arnold. Still others were born in another state, but rose to prominence after becoming citizens of the commonwealth, for example, William Goebel and Jim Porter. Some of the Kentuckians profiled herein played important roles in American history, i.e. Richard M. Johnson. Others, like John Banvard, could only be considered marginally significant. Then there are characters such as Live-Forever Jones, who were in no way notable to history, but lived lives full of entertainment value. They, too, must not be forgotten.

The reader, perhaps having already glanced at the table of contents, may be upset that his or her own favorite offbeat Kentuckian is not in the book. What about Larry Flynt? Hunter S. Thompson?

Gatewood Galbreath? They were certainly offbeat enough to be considered, but I felt arbitrarily that these apologists for illegal drugs and/or pornography simply would not be as much *fun* to write (and read) about as, say, a saloon- smashing lunatic. I also confess to having a preference for writing about 19th and early 20th century personalities, as opposed to still-living persons, perhaps because the full influence of these long-ago figures can be measured. In addition, I wanted to avoid inductees who were too obvious, such as Colonel Sanders. Other Kentuckians, while well known and interesting, did not meet my personal standards for eccentricity in either personality or accomplishments.

If there is a special heaven for Kentuckians (and there ought to be), it's a safe bet Jim Porter is there now, looking down— way down— at Nathan Stubblefield's latest invention. John Shell is comparing notes with Methuselah concerning good places to find senior citizen's discounts. Edgar Cayce is trying to predict how many more years it will be until Speedy Atkins' mortal remains finally decompose. Live-Forever Jones still does not believe he is really dead, and Carry Nation is doing her best to make sure no one is having too much fun.

To Pat Hagen:
Merry Christmas!
— Keven McQueen.
12/12/01

[signature: Kyle McQueen]

Offbeat Kentuckians

by Keven McQueen

Illustrations by Kyle McQueen

McClanahan
Publishing House

International Standard Book Number 0-913383 80 5
Library of Congress Catalog Card Number 2001092283

Cover design and book layout by James Asher Graphics

Manufactured in the United States of America

All book order correspondence should be addressed to:

McClanahan Publishing House, Inc.
P.O. Box 100
Kuttawa, KY 42055
270-388-9388
800-544-6959

www.kybooks.com
books@kybooks.com

Dedicated to my family:

Darrell, Swecia, Kyle, Michael (Lori and Blaine), and Darren

SPECIAL THANKS TO:

Jo Blanset, Lynne Brosius, Drema Colangelo, Paula Cunningham, The Filson Club, Patty Hauck, Charles Hay, Katherine Johnson, The Kentucky Historical Society, Gloria Liss, Barbara McMahon, Kyle McQueen, Theresa Morris, Pat New, Rebecca Rice, Rachael Sadinsky, Meg Shaw, Gaile Sheppard, Mia Temple, Don White. Sorry if I forgot anyone.

Table of Contents

"King" Solomon

Heroic Gravedigger

Times of crisis often bring about unlikely heroes, and Lexington of the 1830s was home to one of the unlikeliest ever: a frowned-upon local vagrant who turned out to be a paragon of selflessness and courage.

His real name was William Solomon, and he had drifted to Lexington sometime in the late 1790s from his home in Virginia. The novelist James Lane Allen described Solomon as being very muscular, over six feet tall, clean-shaven but with long reddish hair and blue eyes. The residents knew little about Solomon except that he was in his early 50s, had more than a passing fondness for alcohol, and performed odd jobs about town in order to pay for his love of drink. His chief means of support was by freelance digging, usually cisterns, graves or cellars. On one occasion when he was especially desperate for libations, Solomon literally sold himself to science by striking a deal with a local physician. It was agreed that in return for a nominal fee, upon his death the doctor would have the use of Solomon's cadaver for medical research.

As is often the case, many locals had little use for an able-bodied man who seemed to prefer drinking to working and who had no visible means of support. Because he was not noted for behaving particularly intelligently while in his cups, Lexington wiseacres bestowed upon

Offbeat Kentuckians

the strapping alcoholic the ironic nickname "King" Solomon after the wisest man in the Old Testament. The name stuck, but if the good-natured idler had any objections to his new identification, there is no record of it.

Solomon's most ignominious public moment occurred on Thursday, June 6, 1833. Local officials had had enough of his vagrancy,

Samuel Woodson Price's portrait of William "King" Solomon, gravedigger and hero.

Courtesy Bodley-Bullock House Museum, Lexington, Ky.

considered a "high misdemeanor" in those days, and ordered him sold as a slave for a period of one year. Sheriff Thomas Brown hauled Solomon to the courthouse steps and offered him to the public at auction as an indentured servant.

James Lane Allen offered an account of the proceedings, perhaps with some artistic license, in his collection of sketches, *Flute and Violin and Other Kentucky Tales.* As told by Allen, most bystanders were amused by the sale, but had no pressing need for an alcoholic handyman. Solomon found himself the subject of derisive comments offered in turn by a tavern keeper, a law student, a farmer and a hatmaker. Someone suggested Solomon be put to use as a scarecrow. Sheriff Brown unbosomed himself of pointed sarcasms about Solomon's ragged clothes, his love for whiskey, his Whig politics and even his homelessness.

At last a hemp factory magnate stepped forward, felt Solomon's muscles, and offered to purchase the man for one dollar. Getting into the spirit of the occasion, two medical students returning from a lecture jestingly bid a dollar and a half. As the auction continued, Solomon displayed only a mild interest in his fate. In the words of writer Ronnie Thompson, "Solomon, ill-kempt and clad in blue jeans and a white cotton shirt, surveyed the crowds calmly while shifting the stump of a cigar in his mouth. When the cigar burned out during the long process of bidding, he immediately produced another, lighted it, and again returned his interest to his own auction."

At length, the bidders had determined Solomon was worth ten dollars. Just as the auction was about to close, a free black woman called Aunt Charlotte approached the crowd. By coincidence, she was also from Virginia and had in fact known Solomon when he was a child. Charlotte, a pie maker by trade, had previously taken pity on Solomon and let him stay in a room in her house on Water Street when he was penniless.

Aunt Charlotte's sympathy for Solomon was rekindled when she saw his humiliating plight. As related by James Lane Allen, she told the sheriff that as white people could purchase blacks to serve as laborers, she thought it fair to buy a white man to work for her.

The ex-slave then offered to buy Solomon for eleven dollars. A student bid twelve dollars. Charlotte made the final winning bid of thirteen dollars, paid it in cash— and then set her servant free, informing him that he could still live in her spare room.

If this unexpected act of kindness put Solomon in a good mood, it was destined not to last very long, for a much larger problem than simply forcing employment upon a vagrant was about to engulf the entire city. The day after Solomon was sold at public auction, Lexington was gripped by an outbreak of Asiatic cholera.

Modern Americans are vaguely familiar with cholera as a disease of long ago that killed people by the score. However, to comprehend what cholera meant to denizens of the 19th century, one must get some idea of how frightening the disease truly was. According to science writer Gina Kolata, "It was a sickness notable for its sudden onset, terrifying and unpredictable spread, and its horrifying mortality. Untreated, cholera kills 40 to 60 percent of its victims." Part of the terror was inspired by the fact that no one was certain how the disease was spread. It is now known that cholera was caused by fecal bacteria that bred in impure drinking water, something found in quantity in those days of poor sanitation and imperfect plumbing. One infected well could affect dozens or even hundreds of people. Writes Kolata, "The bacteria also can be transmitted by food or by flies, on blankets and on clothing." Comparisons to the Black Plague were not unfounded.

And the symptoms! An 1852 article reprinted from a Mississippi newspaper describes what a sufferer from "this terrible scourge of the human race" could expect to undergo: "They are taken with a vomiting and purging of a white serous-looking fluid, resembling rice-water, followed in a short time by violent cramps in the bowels and limbs; these symptoms continue for a short time, when a cold collapsed stage comes on, and in a few hours death closes the horrible scene." The writer's reference to "purging" is a delicate way of mentioning that cholera also produced chronic, dehydrating diarrhea.

On the Thursday he was sold and set free, Solomon scraped up enough cash to buy some liquor. He went to bed thoroughly intoxicated that night, and slept until about 10 a.m. Saturday. When he awoke, Aunt Charlotte told him that one of his friends, a free black barber named Harry Sikes who had often given Solomon free shaves, had died

of cholera and already been buried. Venturing from his room, Solomon found the city a bedlam of the already dead, dying persons afflicted with the loathsome symptoms of cholera, and panic-stricken citizens fleeing Lexington in any possible mode of transportation.

Charlotte was among those eager to flee. She had been loading a wagon with her possessions and urged Solomon to join her as she abandoned the city. Solomon, realizing that his presence might be needed in Lexington, refused to go. Charlotte then vowed that if he wouldn't go, neither would she, and generously gave her wagon to a family so they could leave the city. As it turned out, she survived the epidemic.

Carrying the mattock and spade he often used for odd jobs, Solomon walked through the afflicted city, from Water Street to Mill, and then to Main, all the while watching funeral processions going by, including one heading down Short Street for a French dancing instructor named Adolphe Xaupi who just a couple of nights previously had held a lavish party for Lexington's elite at his Main Street studio.

Wandering to the graveyard on Short Street, Solomon noticed that the coffins of the cholera dead lay unburied; the gravediggers had fled the scene for fear of contracting the contagious disease. At that moment, Solomon knew what he must do. Grabbing his shovel, the laborer began digging graves seemingly with no concern for his own safety.

Considering that an estimated 500 persons died in the epidemic, Solomon had his work cut out for him. He laid out the corpses like a professional mortician and buried some of the people who had tried to buy him as a slave just a few days before. When the hot June sun beat down without mercy, Solomon dug instead in the cool of the night. Allen writes that whenever exhaustion overcame the laborer, he would sleep a while in an unfinished grave.

Deaths from cholera continued well into July, though growing fewer with the passage of time. The June 22 issue of the *Kentucky Gazette* provided a partial list of the dead, along with an explanation for there not having been any issues printed for the previous couple of weeks: too many employees at the newspaper had been ill. On June 29, the *Gazette* noted that "The cholera continues very fatal in the county... We would enforce upon our friends throughout the country, the necessity of continued precaution. Many sudden deaths have resulted from apparently slight indiscretion. Lexington is resuming very slowly some appearance of business."

When the plague had run its course and wary citizens began returning to town, they found that King Solomon, a man scorned and saddled with a sarcastic nickname, had buried their dead for them and by doing so had possibly prevented the epidemic from being worse.

It wasn't long before the Lexingtonians began showing their gratitude. When court sessions resumed, Solomon returned to stand trial for his "high misdemeanor." Instead, the judge, whose wife and daughter had been buried by Solomon, shook his hand. Others attending the court got up to thank Solomon, including the sheriff who sold him and the hemp factory owner who had tried to purchase him.

Solomon lived in Lexington another 21 years, dying in the poorhouse on November 22, 1854, when he was about 73 years old. Although the 1850 Fayette County Census lists him as a pauper, he was still regarded as a folk hero, and the citizenry determined to repay him for his brave services even in death. Solomon's body was carried to Lexington Cemetery in "the finest coffin ever seen in the town." (Obviously the physician who had paid Solomon in advance for medical use of his cadaver never collected.) The former gravedigger was himself buried in a choice spot near the front gates.

In addition, in September 1908, a large tombstone was erected to keep alive the memory of the "Hero of the 1833 cholera plague," as the inscription calls him. One speaker at the ceremony was the celebrated Kentucky artist General Samuel Woodson Price, by then blind, who had personally known Solomon and painted a portrait of the aging vagrant five years before his death. Solomon agreed to sit for the painting as long as Price kept him supplied with cigars and whiskey. (The painting is now on display at the Bodley-Bullock House Museum at 200 Market Street, Lexington.)

At the ceremony the portraitist remarked, "No one living was better acquainted with William Solomon than was I. I know his good qualities, and I was none the less acquainted with his faults. No matter what they may have been, it is the good which should live after men; and I am glad to know that it is still the custom of the people to build monuments of granite and bronze to philanthropists. King Solomon was one. He gave all he possessed for the benefit of mankind— his body and muscle."

Solomon's epitaph even turned around the mocking nature of his nickname by asking, "For had he not a royal heart?"

Richard Mentor Johnson

Vice President

One of Franklin D. Roosevelt's vice presidents, John Nance Garner, famously lamented, "The vice presidency isn't worth a pitcher of warm spit." However, on occasion we encounter a vice president whose performance itself isn't worth a pitcher of warm spit. One of these was Kentucky's Richard M. Johnson.

Johnson was born on October 17, 1780 (some sources claim 1781), when much of Kentucky was still the untamed frontier. The site of his nativity was a settlement called Beargrass, now known more familiarly as Louisville. Shortly thereafter, the family moved first to Bryant's Station, near Lexington, and then to Scott County.

According to relatives, when he was a young man Johnson fell in love with a woman who was either a schoolteacher or a seamstress. He wanted to marry her, but his mother forbade the union. Deeply hurt, Johnson vowed she would regret her interference some day. His revenge was many years delayed, but when it finally came it caused a major political and social scandal.

Johnson's career in politics started normally enough. He attended Transylvania University in Lexington, then afterward studied law. He became a professional lawyer at age 19. Upon developing an interest in politics, he became a member of the General Assembly from 1804-06 and was elected to the House of Representatives in 1807. His career in the House was interrupted by the War of 1812. Johnson, a commissioned Army colonel, led a regiment of volunteers to Canada in 1813, where they fought the British and the Indians. The military engagement that made Colonel Johnson nationally famous was the Battle of the Thames on October 5, 1813. This was the fight that resulted in the death of the Shawnee Indian leader Tecumseh, a figure much feared by settlers.

Johnson was said to have killed Tecumseh, but he was just one of several Indian fighters who took credit for the deed. The real identity of Tecumseh's killer remains a hotly debated historical mystery; the best that can be said for Johnson's claim is that he is as likely to have done it as anybody else. At any rate, the popular assumption that Colonel Johnson was the one who permanently removed the threat of Tecumseh from the frontier certainly did no harm to his political career.

It is true that Johnson behaved with great valor while at war. At the Battle of the Thames, an astonishing 25 bullets allegedly struck either Johnson or his horse, and he had to be carried from the battlefield with wounds in his hip and thigh. When he returned to his seat in the House of Representatives in February 1814, he was lauded as a hero.

Carving of Richard Johnson on his monument in Frankfort Cemetery.
Photo by author.

He remained in the House until 1819, when he was elected to the Senate. For the next several years, until 1837, Johnson was continuous-ly a member of either the Senate or the House. It was said for a while that in Kentucky, Johnson was "more popular even than Henry Clay."

If Johnson had died earlier in his career, he would be remem-bered today as an early American career politician, Kentucky's major Democratic congressman of the early 19th century, and for his bravery in combat. Instead, his political legacy was affected by his personality, which became increasingly erratic and disagreeable with the passage of time, to the point where many observers seriously questioned his sani-ty. Richard Johnson's story becomes a strange one indeed after such a promising beginning.

Unfortunately for his image, Johnson had a talent for repelling others. Described by one observer as "the most vulgar man of all vulgar men in this world," Johnson was notorious for his bad taste in clothing and poor grooming. His personal life became the talk of his enemies and even members of his own party. An unabashed seducer, "he was known to have had sexual flings with the wives of at least four senators and congressmen, and the suspicion existed of at least three more," according to writer Carl Sifakis.

That was just scratching the surface of personal scandal. When his father died, Johnson finally saw his chance to pay his mother back for interfering in his choice of a bride. He inherited a mulatto slave named Julia Chinn, and soon made her his mistress. Johnson was quite open about the well-publicized relationship. He introduced Chinn as his wife (though in actuality Johnson never married), even after he became a Senator and entered Washington society. She bore him two daughters, Adaline and Imogene, whom Johnson insisted on treating as his own legal children, even having them educated and introducing them into society. Both women later married white men and were given generous tracts of land by their father. Furthermore, Scott County court records reveal that he freed many of his other slaves. His open affair with Julia Chinn would return to haunt Johnson repeatedly through his political career by giving his enemies plenty of ammunition with which to attack him, but he never backed down.

But this does not mean Johnson was an especially enlightened man. After Julia died in Lexington's cholera epidemic of 1833, he indulged in relations with a second slave mistress. When the second one ran off with another man, Johnson had her captured and then sold her at auction. Then he made her sister his third mistress.

To be fair, some of Johnson's legislative accomplishments were quite farsighted. He was instrumental in abolishing the debtor's prison in America in 1832 though it took 10 years of constant lobbying, and he made great strides in Indian education. But in keeping with his unstable nature, Johnson also used the Senate floor to discuss strange pet projects. For example, in 1823 he championed the bizarre hollow earth theories of fellow veteran Captain John Cleves Symmes. Johnson even tried to persuade Congress to pass a bill that would fund an expedition to the center of the earth. The bill received only twenty-five votes and was soundly defeated.

In 1836 President Andrew Jackson chose his vice president, Martin Van Buren, to be his successor. The problem was, Van Buren himself would need a vice president. Though by the mid-1830s Congressman Johnson was definitely looking like a liability to his party, he was hand-picked by Jackson himself to be the running mate for Van Buren. (Five years earlier, when Johnson's vice presidential ambitions became known, John Tyler had quipped in reference to the former's habit of using his war wounds to attract votes, "The day is rapidly approaching when an ounce of lead will in truth be worth more than a pound of sense.") Andrew Jackson felt that despite Johnson's antics, his reputation as an Indian fighter and war hero was good for the ticket. Also, he had always been loyal to Jackson, and Jackson was a big believer in the spoils system.

Van Buren did become president in 1837, and vice president Johnson immediately began alienating his peers and the voters with his outrageous behavior. His licentiousness continued unchecked. He cared so little for his duties as vice president that he spent more time at home in Kentucky than in Washington. Indeed, while the country suffered from the financial Panic of 1839, Johnson announced that he was taking a nine-month leave of absence while receiving his full salary.

During this paid vacation, Johnson devoted his energy to opening and publicizing a tavern and spa on his farm in White Sulphur

Spring, Ky. His celebrity drew in many paying customers, one of whom noted in a letter to Amos Kendall, a member of the Van Buren cabinet, "the Vice President of these United States, with all his civic and military honors clustering around his time honored brow, is, or seems to be so happy in the inglorious pursuit of tavern-keeping," and further noted that Johnson seemed preoccupied with nothing more serious than buying eggs and selling watermelons. The suggestion seemed to be that Johnson was much more suited for tavern-keeping than being a heartbeat away from the presidency.

The Democrats finally had enough of Johnson. Even his former supporter Jackson had to admit in a letter to Van Buren that Johnson was "dead weight," and that "...if Col. Johnson is the nominee [for vice president], it will loose [sic] the democracy thousands of votes— jeopardize this state [Tennessee] and surely loose Kentucky... Col. Johnson was the weakest candidate named." When Van Buren ran for re-election in 1839, the party's convention refused to nominate Johnson, or anyone else for that matter, for the vice presidential chair. In other words, Martin Van Buren became the only presidential candidate in American history who had no running mate whatsoever.

A lesser man would have been mortified, but Johnson ran for president himself as an independent candidate. He embarked on a campaign which was highlighted by his bizarre behavior. Even his sympathetic biographer Leland Meyer remarked that "His manners in this most scurrilous campaign in American history were not above reproach." He was criticized for making "incoherent, rambling" speeches. The *Kentucky Gazette* of July 11, 1839, reprinted a report from the *Scioto Gazette* claiming that while stumping in Ohio, Johnson displayed his battle scars to the audience. The article also delivered a few tongue-in-cheek compliments: "What though he does crave credit for valiant feats he never performed, has he no precedent for it? ....What if he did not write [the famous Sunday Mail Report]? It requires a man of some ingenuity to palm off the production of another as his own."

During that campaign of 1840, the memorable Whig slogan was "Tippecanoe and Tyler, too." Someone in the Johnson camp— some have suggested it was Johnson himself— reflected that their candidate was himself a hero of the War of 1812, and composed a rival campaign slogan: "Rumpsey dumpsey, Rumpsey dumpsey! Colonel Johnson killed Tecumseh!" (However, there is evidence the slogan existed as early as 1824.) This campaign jingle is fondly remembered by historians as one of the most moronic ever devised. Johnson was trounced at the polls, receiving only 48 electoral votes. The crowning embarrassment was that he did not carry Kentucky, his home state.

Richard Johnson returned to Congress in 1841, but again attempted unsuccessfully to run for president in 1844. After this defeat, he retired to his tavern in Kentucky. In 1850 he was elected once more to the House of Representatives.

However, though elected he was unable to serve. His long-standing erratic behavior had finally turned into outright mental illness. The Frankfort correspondent for the *Louisville Daily Journal* of November 9, 1850, informed its readership: "Col. R.M. Johnson is laboring under an attack of dementia, which renders him totally unfit for business. It is painful to see him on the floor attempting to discharge the duties of a member. He is incapable of properly exercising his physical or mental powers. The veteran form that has filled so many important posts in civil life and born itself so gallantly upon the battle field seems to totter, and the mind which vivified it seems to flicker and wane in a dim uncertain light."

Richard Johnson died in Frankfort of a stroke on November 19, 1850. His uniqueness lives after him: he remains the only vice president who was so unpopular that he was elected to the office by Congress rather than by popular vote, in accordance with Amendment XII of the Constitution.

Jim Porter and Martin Van Buren Bates

Two Kentucky Giants

We are surrounded by tall people. Thanks to improvements in nutrition, since the turn of the last century humans have been getting taller with each generation. And yet, persons over six and a half feet in height are still uncommon enough to evoke surprise and wonder. Imagine, then, how a person of that height, or even taller, would seem in the mid-19th century, when the average man ranged from five-feet-six to five-feet-eight inches and most women were a little over five feet tall. Abraham Lincoln, for one, was considered extremely tall at six-feet-four. Perhaps this puts a little perspective on the noteworthiness of two Kentuckians from that era, Jim Porter and Martin Van Buren Bates, who were each well over *seven* feet tall.

The first, James D. Porter, was known in his time as the Louisville Giant. He was born in Portsmouth, Ohio, on December 15, 1811. (Some sources give the year 1810, but this is the date on Porter's gravestone.) When he was still a baby, his family moved to the Louisville neighborhood of Shippingport.

Nothing in Porter's childhood suggested that he would ever become a giant; quite the opposite, in fact. He was sickly and under-sized as a child, so much so that around age 14 he was in training to be a jockey at a racetrack near Louisville's Elm Tree Garden.

His phenomenal growth began when he was 17 years old. Indeed, he grew with such rapidity that neighbors insisted on measuring him every Saturday, as his increasing height was a subject of their wagering. Allegedly he once grew an inch in a single week. At age 21 he was six-feet-nine, and when he stopped growing around age 25 he was seven-feet-nine, or as Porter liked to say, "six feet, 21 inches." He was supposedly the tallest known man in the world at the time.

In his prime, Porter weighed 300 pounds. A portrait in the possession of the Filson Club reveals that he had surrealistically massive hands; they were 13 inches from base of palm to tip of middle finger. The club also owns a cast of his left hand, proving that the painter of the portrait did not exaggerate.

Obviously, a giant requires larger-than-average accouterments. Porter owned a 95-inch-long shotgun and a sword five feet long, both given to him by a manufacturer in Springfield, Mass. The Filson Club owns the rifle and one of his boots, slightly over 14 inches high. Collins' *History of Kentucky* notes that Porter walked with a spiral four-and-a-half-foot cane that resembled a bedpost.

The Louisville Giant could have made a fortune by exhibiting himself with traveling carnivals, but he refused almost every offer. Instead, he tried to make an honest living as a cooper, and then by driving a coach. In 1836 he opened a modest inn near the Portland Canal locks, and steamboat travelers from Cincinnati, Pittsburgh and New Orleans were eager to do business at the tavern in order to see its enormous proprietor.

Porter was so well-known by the late 1830s that when Charles Dickens toured America for the purpose of writing his travel book *American Notes* (1842), he made sure to see the giant when he reached Louisville. Legend has it that when Dickens imperiously sent word for Porter to meet him aboard a steamboat, Porter sent this testy rebuff: "Tell Charles Dickens Jim Porter is a bigger sight than Charles Dickens," after which the novelist humbly met Porter at his tavern. However, if this exchange actually took place, Dickens does not mention it in his book. Instead, after noting that real giants are almost invariably gentle and mild-mannered, Dickens describes his encounter

Offbeat Kentuckians

with Porter, which contrary to legend seems indeed to have taken place aboard a steamboat:

"He had a weakness in the region of the knees, and a trustfulness in his long face, which appealed even to five-feet-nine for encouragement and support. He was only twenty-five years old, he said, and had grown recently, for it had been found necessary to make an addition to the legs of his inexpressibles. At fifteen he was a short boy, and in those days his English father and his Irish mother had rather snubbed him, as being too small of stature to sustain the credit of the family. He added that his health had not been good, though it was better now; but short people are not wanting who whisper that he drinks too hard.

"I understand he drives a hackney-coach, though how he does it, unless he stands on the footboard behind, and lies along the roof upon his chest, with his chin in the box, it would be difficult to comprehend. He brought his gun with him, as a curiosity. Christened 'The Little Rifle,' and displayed outside a shop-window, it would make the

Jim Porter, the Kentucky Giant. *Courtesy Filson Club Historical Society, Louisville, Ky.*

fortune of any retail business in Holborn. When he had shown himself and talked a little while, he withdrew with his pocket-instrument, and went bobbing down the cabin, among men of six feet high and upwards, like a lighthouse walking among lamp-posts."

Porter's only known attempt to publicly exploit his height was when he was talked into performing for a year (1836-37) as the title character in a traveling road show of *Gulliver's Travels.* A couple of dwarves were also in the play, portraying Lilliputians. Porter must not have been impressed with life on the road, as he later turned down numerous lucrative offers to perform, even rejecting that greatest of showmen, P.T. Barnum.

Porter was known throughout Louisville for his kind nature, "modest and retiring— the very soul of honor and honesty," as the *Daily Courier's* eulogy phrased it. Politically, he was a Whig and an admirer of Henry Clay. It has been said that whenever Porter walked the streets, a long line of youngsters would follow their friendly giant. That he was a children's favorite is confirmed by A.J. Webster, who in 1930 wrote his reminiscences of growing up in Louisville for the Filson Club: "One of the things that the boys appreciated about as much as a circus was the Kentucky Giant— Jim Porter. Almost any day he could be seen driving on Main Street in his one-seat buggy, a big mule pulling it, and his knees higher than the dashboard. He always dressed in a long-tail frock coat, an old-fashioned standing collar and a high hat. I have forgotten his height, but I recall he had a measuring competition with the much advertised 'P.T. Barnum's giant,' and he overtopped him by several inches."

Sadly, Porter's reach exceeded his grasp when in 1847 he decided to build a newer, larger combined tavern and hotel with his earnings. The new 18-room establishment was located on Front Street in Shippingport, but it was a financial failure as the burgeoning railroad industry began luring away steamboat passengers. To make matters worse, Porter's health began to fail. He suffered especially from heart troubles and inflammatory rheumatism. But even in this time of poor health and monetary distress, Porter had too much pride to make a quick dollar by exploiting his height before the curious.

On April 25, 1859, the Louisville Giant was found dead in bed when relatives went to wake him for breakfast. He died of a heart attack, possibly brought on by stress caused by his financial predicament. He was only 47 years old.

Porter was laid to rest in a specially-made casket slightly over nine feet long and two feet wide at the breast. Covered with black cloth and lined with white satin, the coffin "attracted more attention than anything of the kind that ever enclosed the lifeless remains of one of our citizens," as a local newspaper quaintly noted. In 1937, an 85-year-old Louisville resident named William Carnes Kendrick mentioned in his memoirs that the undertaker, Mr. Wyatt, exhibited the empty casket to the curious, at one point placing his 10-year-old daughter inside "that those present might see the contrast in sizes between child and giant."

Once Porter's body was placed in the casket, the funeral procession, which consisted of 40 carriages, carried him to a vault in Cave Hill Cemetery. Kendrick remembered that visitors could peek through the vault's ornamental metal door and see the giant's stone sarcophagus, beside which was placed a coffin of ordinary size for comparative purposes. Many years later, Porter's immense casket was removed from the vault and buried in a nearby plot. Other monuments in the cemetery may be taller, but certainly none of the graves are longer than his.

The second noted Kentucky giant was Martin Van Buren Bates, born in Whitesburg, Letcher County, on November 9, 1845, the youngest of 11 children. His parents, according to an 1896 book on medical curiosities by Doctors Gould and Pyle, were very much of average size. Bates's father, John W. Bates of Virginia, was five-feet-ten and

Two Kentucky Giants

Two married giants: Anna Swan and Kentucky's Martin Van Buren Bates, 7'5" and 7'2" respectively. The man at the far right is 6'2".
From *The Kentucky River Giant.*

his mother Sarah was five-feet-three. And yet they somehow produced a son who was slightly over seven-feet-two and weighed 450 pounds when he ceased growing.

The young giant was attending Emory and Henry College in Virginia when the Civil War disrupted his academic career. Bates joined the Fifth Kentucky Infantry of the Confederate Army under Col. John S. Williams in September 1861; after receiving several promotions, on November 14, 1863, he became a first lieutenant in Company A of the Virginia State Line Troops. Eventually this company merged into the Seventh Confederate Cavalry. (One can only wonder how he must have appeared galloping across a battlefield astride a horse.) The outfit specialized in chasing guerrillas, nearly wiping out one especially violent band that preyed on citizens near the Virginia-Kentucky border. By the time the war was over, Bates was a captain. His authentic military rank came in handy later, when he would be displayed in full uniform to impressed audiences.

After the war, Bates moved to Cincinnati and took advantage of his great height by joining various circuses and traveling shows as an exhibition, starting with the Wiggins and Bennoitt show for $100 per month in July 1865. Soon afterwards he joined the John Robinson circus for quadruple his former salary. In contrast to Jim Porter, Bates greatly enjoyed performing and touring. Between 1866 and 1880, he journeyed all over the United States, and also in Canada, Great Britain, France, Spain, Germany, Switzerland, Austria and Russia, according to Gould and Pyle.

While on one of these tours, Captain Bates met Anna Swan, a young giantess from New Annan, Nova Scotia, who measured a formidable seven-feet-five. Of Swan's parents, only her father was of slightly above-average height at six feet; her mother was five-feet-two. Like her husband, Swan experienced rapid growth in childhood; she weighed 18 pounds at birth, was as tall as her mother at age six, and was over seven feet tall at age 15. By the time Bates met her, Swan had already had a long career with P.T. Barnum, and once in New York she acted in a production of *Macbeth*. She was surely the largest Lady Macbeth in theatrical history.

The captain and Anna Swan were soon paired up onstage. While on a tour of London, the giants twice gave a command performance before Queen Victoria. Their act usually consisted of such elegancies as reciting monologues and dramatic readings.   B a t e s was taken with Swan, who had been described by her promoter Barnum as "intelligent and by no means ill-looking." Finding they had more in common than just their vertical altitude, the couple were married at Saint-Martin's-in-the-Field, London, on June 17, 1871, becoming "the tallest married couple known to mankind," with a combined height of 14 feet and eight inches. Anna's bridal gown required 100 yards of white satin and 50 yards of lace. Queen Victoria bestowed wedding presents upon both the captain and his bride: he received an engraved watch and chain, and Anna was given a cluster diamond ring.

Sideshow promoters were not long in realizing that the only draw better than a giant is two married giants. The Bateses became a popular traveling attraction, performing before the Prince and Princess of Wales, Grand Duke Vladimir of Russia, Prince John of Luxembourg, and of course vast audiences of delighted common folk, as well.

After the couple earned enough money to live comfortably, in July 1874 they retired temporarily from show business to a 130-acre farm in Seville, Medina County, Ohio, where the captain became noted for his prize cattle and draft horses. He also built an 18-room mansion fit for a giant, complete with doorways over eight feet high, ceilings ranging in height from eight to 14 feet, and huge furniture custom made for the Bateses. Their bed was 10 feet long and twice as high as an average bed. Anna was proud owner of a dressing table that, according to one account, held a mirror almost as large as the side of an ordinary room. Adding to this scene of large-scale domestic bliss, the couple became members of the local Baptist church, where they sat in specially-made pews.

However, the lure of show business was strong, and the couple went on tour with the Cole Brothers Circus from 1878 to 1880. During this engagement, the Bateses suffered a domestic tragedy. Anna, who had previously given birth to a stillborn baby on May 19, 1872, found that she was again pregnant. After an extremely difficult labor, on January 19, 1879, Mrs. Bates gave birth to the largest baby recorded in medical history up to that time. According to the attending surgeon, the newborn boy was 30 inches long and weighed nearly 24 pounds. His head had an incredible 19-inch circumference. The child died the same day he was born, and was buried in Mound Hill Cemetery near Seville. (According to author Frederick Drimmer, the Medina County Historical Society possesses a photo of the colossal baby, and the Cleveland Health Museum displays a life-size plaster cast of the child.)

Heartbroken, the Bateses finished out the circus' 1880 season, but then retired to their Ohio farm permanently. They were much loved by the community, and for years a local attraction was a floor that collapsed when the couple danced on it.

Bates spent some time writing an autobiography entitled *The Kentucky River Giant*. The brief but well-written book was composed sometime after 1879 but published posthumously, and is now a rarity. The captain's touching professions of love for his wife figure prominently in his memoirs. In the preface, he states: "I cannot conclude without endeavoring in some small degree to testify my unbounded love for the wife that seems to have been created for me. To her kindness, her intelligence, her religious and ever faithful care I owe a debt that even life cannot repay."

After nearly a decade of an idyllic existence, tragedy again entered the captain's life. Anna died of a heart condition on August 5, 1888; had she lived but one more day, she would have been forty-two. Drimmer relates that the captain ordered a custom-sized casket from a Cleveland manufacturer but since the company thought the instructions must be in error, a coffin of ordinary dimensions arrived. Anna Bates' funeral was one of the best-attended in the history of the community, but it had to be delayed until an appropriate casket could be made.

After two years of being a widower, in 1890 the captain married a woman named Anne Lavonne Weatherby of Cincinnati, five feet tall, whose father was the pastor at the local Baptist church. Bates himself died on January 14, 1919, and like his first wife's funeral, his own had some touches of grim humor. Long before his death, the captain had a gigantic brass casket made for himself which he stored in his barn. It was decided that the requested six pallbearers were not sufficient to carry the load, so eight were employed instead. However, the casket was much too long to fit in the hearse, and the back door of the vehicle had to be tied open. Captain Bates and his wife are buried in the family plot in Mound Hill Cemetery along with their child.

According to Drimmer, nothing is left of the Bateses' overscaled mansion. Subsequent owners of average size found it just too large, so "it was torn down in 1948, and much of the lumber used to build a new dwelling on the site. Only Bates's barn is left, with his name painted on the roof." A melancholy ending indeed for a very large house that was once called home by a very large Kentuckian.

John Banvard

Artist

Young John Banvard had artistic talent; everyone agreed on that. Some felt his art was better than average, while others believed he lacked that touch of genius that would elevate his work from the agreeably competent into the realm of the immortal. Perhaps no one who knew him, however, could have predicted that some day he would create a painting with such a staggering concept behind it that until recently no artist, even those with more talent, came even close to equaling it.

Banvard was born in New York City on November 15, 1815. His faculty for drawing was marked early in his life and as recently as 1958 some of his childhood sketches still existed. When he was only 16 years old, he moved to Louisville, Ky., which became the base of his artistic activities. Before becoming a professional painter, Banvard worked as a clerk in a drugstore, but his boss fired him due to his propensity for drawing caricatures on the walls of the establishment. Banvard entered a financially precarious period of taking art lessons, painting scenic backdrops for a theater and doing artwork for hire. At one point he and several friends rode a flatboat down the Ohio and Mississippi Rivers to New Orleans, a trip that left him greatly impressed with the scenery along the route. During the voyage he also used the flatboat as a sort of mobile art gallery where he exhibited and tried to sell his paintings. This was followed by an itinerant life in which Banvard painted for theaters at Natchez, New Orleans, Cincinnati and Louisville. He also succeeded in selling some of his panoramic land-scapes.

Back home, an idea formed in the young artist's mind to create a painting on a gigantic scale such as the world had never seen before. But what subject would be grand enough to match the enormity of Banvard's vision? The answer was perhaps obvious to a citizen of Louisville who was treated daily to the sight of steamboats coming and going, being loaded and unloaded by colorful dockworkers, and the passengers of every imaginable description who embarked and disem-barked. He would paint a landscape of the Mississippi River. All of it, from one end to the other.

In 1840 the ambitious Banvard began his project by making sketches around Louisville. Using his savings of $3,000, he then took a trip on a raft to explore the entire river all the way down to New Orleans, painstakingly drawing thousands of pictures of the scenery all the while. It was by no means a pleasure trip. The artist suffered from perpetual sunburn, had to hunt and forage for his meals and slept on sandbars. A portfolio served both as a repository for his sketches and as a pillow at night. Banvard later wrote that he "had to travel thousands of miles alone in an open skiff, crossing and recrossing the rapid stream, in many places over two miles in breadth, to select proper points of sight from which to take his sketch." Anyone who has read Mark Twain's *Life On The Mississippi* is aware of the myriad hazards a trip down the river could provide even for a large steamboat, and will appre-ciate Banvard's solo feat in accomplishing the same 2,000-mile route in a tiny skiff.

The voyage took over a year. When Banvard returned to Kentucky in 1841, he had a studio constructed on the outskirts of Louisville and started working on his painting, titled "Moving Panorama of the Mississippi River," on a canvas 12 feet high and 1,320 feet long, specially made by a firm in Lowell, Mass. Banvard did all the painting himself with no aid from assistants. Five years after it was begun, the landscape depicted 1,200 miles of the mighty river and its shoreline from New Orleans to the mouth of the Missouri. The paint-

ing was spectacularly detailed, featuring all major cities on the route including Natchez, Memphis and St. Louis, in addition to minor settlements, plantations, and small farms. The spectator was treated to majestic steamboats, flatboats, keelboats, trade boats, boats of every kind, and beautiful forests of various trees including cypress, sycamore, oak, magnolia, and cottonwood. The painting also depicted sandbars, islands, forts, Indian villages, high cliffs, swamps, animal life, changes in weather, a shipwreck, and humans going about their daily routines along the way. Critics would later praise the colors of the painting, the natural and varied lighting effects and the cloud groupings in the sky. The landscape even depicted sunrise and nightfall, in order to show the beauty of the river at all times of day.

John Banvard, laboring in his Louisville studio, had successfully completed the largest painting ever made up to that time. He felt the painting was unfinished but decided to exhibit it in order to make enough capital to complete the project. Banvard had to invent a unique method for displaying such an enormous picture to an audience. The canvas would be wrapped around a giant upright cylinder, then slowly unrolled onto another cylinder by two uniformed attendants. The entire exhibition would take over two hours.

On June 29, 1846, the painting received its first public display during a week's showing at the Apollo Rooms, admission 50 cents a head, children and servants half price. The enthusiastic local press touted the work, claiming erroneously that the canvas was three miles long (a mistake that became an oft-repeated part of the painting's legend, but also a mistake Banvard was understandably happy to encourage). The *Morning Courier,* for example, called the painting "one of the greatest achievements of industry and genius on record," and said it appealed to civic pride: "As a Louisvillian we are proud of Mr. Banvard, and we hope our citizens will show their appreciation of his talents and unconquerable industry... Mr. B. has spent thousands of dollars in this city in getting this great work ready, and well does he deserve remuneration." A handbill was circulated about town listing some of the scenes depicted in the painting, but added, "Any description of this leviathan picture that should be attempted in a bill like this would convey but a faint idea of what it really is."

Opening night was as disastrous as a Mississippi steamboat wreck. Banvard later stated not one person was in attendance due to stormy weather; his claim is verified by the *Morning Courier* of June 30. In desperation, the artist gave out free tickets to men who worked on the river. They attended the second night's showing, and the trick worked. The river men, "astonished by its accuracy and beauty," quickly spread word of the remarkable painting to anyone who would listen. On July 1 the *Morning Courier* referred to it as "the greatest and proudest work of art *in the world!*" By the end of the week, the auditorium was so crowded with citizens who had to see the massive artwork for themselves, including approving riverboat pilots, that the exhibition was extended two more days.

Banvard took the profits and worked on the panorama three more months. When he displayed it again in October, the artist was lauded by the press, the mayor, the Kentucky Historical Society and by the public, which enriched Banvard several thousand dollars with ticket sales. By this time, citizens of other cities were clamoring to see the great work and the artist decided to take it on a tour of the United States.

The exhibition of the painting itself increased in sophistication after its debut; as an orchestra played and the artist himself lectured the audience, the canvas was slowly unspooled by a machine that turned the cylinders. The "Panorama" arrived in Boston in December 1846, where it was so popular it was shown for nearly an entire year at Amory Hall. The theater was filled to capacity almost every day, and indeed on some days up to 500 disappointed patrons had to be turned away. Railway companies ran special trains just for crowds who came to Boston to see Banvard's landscape. It was later calculated that an average of 1,165 viewers saw the "Panorama" daily. Banvard took his painting to New York City, between $50,000 and $75,000 richer for his efforts in Boston. And he received a reward on a personal, as opposed to financial, level; he married a young lady named Elizabeth Goodnow, who had been hired to play piano as the landscape's scenery unfolded.

A building was constructed in New York for the sole purpose of displaying the "Panorama." In that city the painting was immensely popular, as in Boston. Most of those who saw Banvard's artwork regarded it as more than a curiosity, a freakishly large picture. For many, it was "emblematical of the spirit of America," in the words of the *New York Herald*. Before Banvard, American artists suffered from what might be called an inferiority complex on a global scale. But at last, the new nation had produced a work that even the finest painters of Europe had to acknowledge held a unique position in the world of art. Banvard became a folk hero, and to many he and his painting *were* America. His engagingly folksy narration to the audience as the painting slowly passed by was considered as much of an attraction as the artwork itself.

Like any artist, Banvard had the desire to constantly improve his masterpiece. While in New York in 1848, he painted and added another lengthy section to the "Panorama" featuring part of the Missouri River, one of the Mississippi's two main tributaries. The new section delineated the Missouri's path from the point where it joined the Mississippi up to the Rocky Mountains. The painting now depicted 2,300 miles of river landscape from the Rockies to New Orleans, including Indian encampments, Indians doing war dances and hunting bison, views of the plains (including a prairie fire) and varied rock formations.

After making an additional $40,000 to $50,000 in New York, Banvard headed for Liverpool, England, with his improved "Panorama" in September 1848. The massive work went on public display in London's Egyptian Hall, Piccadilly, in December. It played for a year and a half, and in an era when any artifact of American culture was often treated with suspicion or condescension in the European press, the reviews were enthusiastic, though British critics did find some fault with the execution of the artwork. The cavils of critics seemed powerless when, in April 1849, Queen Victoria and Prince Albert saw the "Panorama" at St. George's Hall. After the performance, Her Majesty remarked that she wished Banvard were a British subject so she could give him a knighthood.

As the riches poured in from British audiences, Banvard completed one more stretch of scenery for the landscape in early 1849. This time he added some of the west bank of the Mississippi and a large section of the Ohio River, the Mississippi's other major tributary. The newest section was at least 900 feet long. The Ohio River section of the painting depicted such wonders as the construction of a flatboat, a timber raft, atmospheric river fog, the grave of President William Henry Harrison on a hilltop, a steamboat being loaded with wood, a forest fire, a log cabin, a mail steamer and various cities along the route including Cincinnati and New Albany, In. Most critics agreed that Banvard's artistic skills grew with each new section of the grand "Panorama."

Partly to stave off competition from other panoramists, Banvard decided to show two sections of his work separately; one city would see the east bank of the Mississippi and the Missouri River, while elsewhere he displayed the west bank of the Mississippi and the Ohio. The earlier panorama went on to do excellent business in Scotland, France, then Britain again. The landscape of the Mississippi and the Ohio remained in Britain, touring the smaller towns. In September 1850, Banvard at last combined all the paintings, and the work was renamed "Moving Panorama of the Mississippi, Missouri, and Ohio Rivers." The finished landscape was more than 3,000 feet long as it was slowly unfurled on its cylinders. (The *Guinness Book of Records* claimed the painting's length was closer to 5,000 feet which, if true, meant it was nearly a mile long when completed.)   It went on to tour England, Scotland and Ireland for two more years. Since the complete work covered over 3,000 miles across 12 American states, it made for a very long performance, but no one seemed to mind.

John Banvard returned to America around 1852, leaving the "Panorama" to tour Europe with a replacement narrator as he worked in New York on his new project, a landscape of the Nile River, Egypt and Israel, which featured various sites mentioned in the Bible. This painting was also enormous; it was forty-eight feet high and covered more than 1,200 square feet. Like the paintings of the Mississippi, Banvard's Holy Land panorama was an enormous financial success. It underwent extensive touring, and over the years he added to its length.

Eventually the landscape of the Mississippi returned to America, where Banvard continued to update it and display it to the public annually, though its popularity was now superseded by that of the artist's Holy Land panorama. In 1862 he added Civil War battles to the Mississippi River scenery. Interestingly, Banvard's experience with the Mississippi proved to be helpful to the war effort. The artist drew a chart for Union General Fremont showing how Island No.10 in the river could be passed by taking a circuitous route through a canal and some bayous. Fremont followed the suggestion to great success.

In 1867 Banvard bought some land in New York City and built a theater and museum at 1221 Broadway where the "Panorama" was put on display. (Some sources claim he did not show the painting there, but it seems hard to believe he would pass an opportunity to exhibit his most celebrated work.) He called the building Banvard's Museum and attempted to model it after the famous Barnum's Museum. He failed at this enterprise, and after changing hands a couple of times the building became known as Daly's Theater. The artist had amassed a great fortune from his painting over the years— by one estimate about $200,000, but he lost most of it in the financial panics of the 1870s. One of his final exhibitions of the great landscape was made in New York in April 1881.

In addition to his panoramas, Banvard made other contributions to art and literature. He composed over 1,700 poems, several hundred of which were published in America and Great Britain. He wrote at least two plays which were enacted onstage, *Amasis, or The Last of the Pharaohs* (c.1864) and *Carrinia* (c.1875). One of his non-panoramic paintings, "The Orison," had the honor of being the first picture from which a chromo made in America was taken. (These were a form of color lithograph and quite the rage in the late 19th century. For a contemporary reference to chromos, see chapter 32 of Mark Twain's *Life on the Mississippi*.)

Despite all his success, Banvard retired from the art world and moved with his family to Watertown, S. D., in July 1883. He brought the Mississippi panorama with him and kept it in a local storage house. Banvard died on May 16, 1891, at age 76, and was buried in Watertown's Mount Hope Cemetery. He was lauded in obituaries across the nation, but few today have heard of either Banvard or his painting of unsurpassed dimensions. Two of his modern biographers perhaps said it best when they dryly commented, "Quantitatively, John Banvard was the world's greatest artist."

Banvard's record stood unchallenged for nearly 150 years. However, in 1990 an Australian artist named Ken Done supervised a painting on canvas measuring 72,347 square feet, making his the largest painting of all time. It is worth noting that the Australian painting was a group effort, consisting of hundreds of squares painted by college students and a number of school children. By contrast, Banvard's painting was created with no assistants.

Alas for posterity, the whereabouts of the original Banvard landscape is a mystery. It may seem improbable that something so massive could just disappear, but that is the case. The *Guinness Book of Records* claimed the painting was stored in a barn at Cold Spring Harbor, Long Island, N.Y., and was destroyed in a fire, but Banvard's family stated that they last saw it in the warehouse in Watertown. It has been speculated that the "Panorama" was cut into pieces and used as backdrops in South Dakota theaters, but surely that could not account for all 3,000 feet of the painting. The only hints we have of the painting's visual greatness are verbal descriptions from playbills and reviews, preliminary sketches made by Banvard that are still in existence, and some engravings of various scenes made by the British press. It is possible that pieces of Banvard's masterpiece do still exist, but simply are not recognized as being portions of the painting that once stunned two continents and made its creator one of the most famous men in America.

Alexander McClung

Duelist

In the popular imagination, the stereotypical Kentucky gentleman of the 19th century wore a snow-white suit complete with broad hat and string tie, sported a fine goatee, and fought duels at the slightest provocation. Alexander Keith McClung had no goatee and wore no white suit, but he more than lived up to expectations as far as his dueling pistols were concerned.

Stereotypes aside, McClung's life was colorful and violent. He was born in Virginia in 1811, scion of a prominent family that soon moved to Washington, Mason County, Ky. (On the other hand, some sources claim he was born in Mason County in 1812.) His father William was a judge who had studied law with Thomas Jefferson. His older brother was John A. McClung, Presbyterian minister and noted author; his uncle was Chief Justice James Marshall of Virginia, and he was a cousin to the aristocratic Breckinridges. Early on, however, Alexander McClung seemed determined to strike out on his own. He left home for Brooklyn and there he joined the Navy, being commissioned as a midshipman on April 1, 1828.

His bunkmate was Benjamin Sands, later to become a rear admiral. He recalled in his autobiography that even at this tender age, McClung seemed to have a pathological temper and was constantly getting into fights and threatening others over imagined slights. On one cruise, McClung managed the feat of having to fight duels with two separate crewmates in a single day. In the first affray, which took place ashore in Montevideo, he ended up with a broken arm but managed to shoot off his opponent's thumb. The second duel never took place. Though McClung was eager to prove his mettle after his arm healed, the Navy had already had quite enough of his bellicosity and forced him to resign on August 20, 1829, after serving a little over a year.

Back in Kentucky, McClung entered an inconclusive duel in Frankfort with his cousin James W. Marshall. McClung's love for fighting with pistols was by now approaching a mania. He solemnly promised his concerned Calvinist mother that he would never again challenge another man to a duel. Instead, he worked hard at cultivating a personality so obnoxious others would challenge him first.

In 1833, having already frivoled away his inheritance, McClung took to the road again at age 22. He drifted to Jackson, Miss., where he made a halfhearted attempt at becoming a lawyer in between duels. Much later, in 1846, he fought gallantly in the Mexican War.

But it was neither sailoring nor soldiering, nor even his lawyering, that caused McClung to be feared far and wide. He had a taste for alcohol, and when under the influence he was apt to threaten anyone who displeased him and try to trick the unfortunates into challenging him to duels. Because McClung was an expert shot, he was always the participant left standing. His nephew John Henderson McClung estimated that in all he fought 14 duels and killed 10 opponents on the field of honor. McClung's fights made him such a legendary figure that he made his mark in the world of literature; the character Keith Alexander in James Street's 1942 novel *Tap Roots* is based on McClung.

McClung's earliest notable duel took place in 1834, only a few months after he moved to Mississippi. He had an argument with a lawyer friend, General Allen of Jackson, and inevitably the challenge was made to the hotheaded young Kentuckian. The conditions McClung set were bizarre. The antagonists were to stand 80 paces apart, armed with a bowie knife and four dueling pistols apiece, and walk towards each other while firing at will. If they ran out of bullets, they were to fight with the knives, which meant it was a foregone conclusion someone was going to be killed. As the former friends approached each other on the bank of the Pearl River, McClung fired a shot that seemed miraculous; at a distance of 100 feet he fatally shot Allen through the teeth. In the words of Robert Baldick, who wrote a history of dueling, "The distance from which McClung fired was a much longer range than that for which dueling pistols were intended, and his mortal shot created a sinister record, at the same time establishing his reputation as one of the most dangerous men in the South."

The duelist was soon given the sobriquet "The Black Knight of the South." He did his best to look the part. He was over six feet tall, thin, clean-shaven, red-haired, and his clothing marked him as a dandy. Often he wore a foppish flowing cape, beneath which he was well-armed against all challengers. He enjoyed taking a theatrical approach to life and behaved as if he were an actor on stage, even affecting a fondness for poetry.

As both his reputation and alcoholism grew, so inevitably did McClung's penchant for bullying. Baldick writes that as the duelist's body count grew, "the mere mention of his name was enough to unnerve the bravest of men." On one occasion when he was staying at a hotel, another guest had the effrontery to complain to the waiter when McClung stuck his knife in the butter. The duelist countered by smearing butter in the guest's face while complaining mockingly, "Waiter, remove the butter— this man has stuck his nose in it." The guest handed McClung his card as a prelude to a duel, and promptly received one in return. Upon glancing at the card and discovering he had just challenged the Black Knight, the would-be combatant blanched and stammered, "Just let me have my card back, that's all I ask." McClung indulgently did so, according to at least some accounts.

Such events render ludicrous a flattering profile of McClung that appeared in the *Southern Literary Messenger* shortly before the duelist's death, which included the words "He is the last man among all we have known, who would condescend to seek *notoriety,* or to feign a resentment he does not feel." To the contrary, obviously McClung reveled in his notoriety and went about looking for trouble.

At one point McClung fell in love with Virginia Tunstall, a belle of Tuscaloosa, Al., and from her we gain more evidence of the famous duelist's mental instability. She wrote that he suffered from periods of

Alexander Keith
McClung.
*Courtesy State
Historical
Museum/Mississippi
Department of
Archives and History.*

the blackest depression (perhaps he suffered from what we now know to be manic depression). Sometimes he would mount his horse Rob Roy and dash to the cemetery, where he would lay outstretched on a grave and stare "like a madman into the sky." One afternoon he took Virginia for a ride along the riverside in his carriage and proposed marriage by romantically threatening to drive into the river and drown them both if she refused. She agreed, only to change her mind the next morning.

Meanwhile, the violence that followed McClung everywhere continued. He met another Kentuckian who moved to Mississippi, a planter and merchant named John Menefee (brother of Congressman Richard Menefee, after whom Menifee County would later be named, albeit with a misspelling). The two became close friends, but one day when they went swimming in the Pearl River, some youths hid their clothes as a practical joke. Menefee caught one of them and commenced giving him a sound thrashing. McClung objected, and as a result he and Menefee got into a fight. Their hard feelings led to a later brawl in a pool hall, during the course of which Menefee bashed McClung over the head with a cue. For the first time in years McClung himself challenged someone to a duel.

On December 29, 1839, the two met on Dueling Island at Vicksburg for the purpose of settling their differences with a pair of Mississippi rifles rather than the standard dueling pistols. It promised to be an even fight, for once, as Menefee was a soldier who also had a reputation as a crack shot, especially with a rifle. At the agreed-upon distance of 60 yards, the pair turned and faced each other. Menefee fired first, but the ball narrowly missed McClung and struck only a tree. McClung's rifle "hung fire," so instead of killing his opponent, he tried in a rage to break his weapon in half, then swore a furious oath and tossed the gun aside into a pile of sand. But the encounter was far from over. McClung's seconds retrieved the rifle, cleaned and reloaded it, and handed it back to him. The two duelists resumed their positions as the vast crowd of onlookers wagered on the outcome.

Those who bet on Menefee were to head home poorer. Before the planter could fire for a second time, McClung shot off a piece of Menefee's own rifle. The ball split in half and a stray chunk of metal entered the unfortunate man's forehead. He expired within moments. After performing this feat of marksmanship, McClung's high-handed arrogance bloomed in full. Ever fond of dramatic, theatrical gestures, he dropped to his knees, fondled and kissed his rifle, and loudly thanked God "for having directed the bullet so well." Even in a society in which dueling was a fact of life, this gloating was considered unbecoming.

McClung fought few if any duels in his later years, largely because he could find no one who would fight him under any circumstances. His bloodlust had to be satisfied by more conventional violence when he entered the Mexican War as lieutenant colonel in the First Mississippi Regiment. As might be expected, he fought boldly and recklessly and was wounded at Buena Vista. During the the Battle of Monterrey in September 1846, he was the first to scale the Mexican battlements. He planted the Stars and Stripes, but as he did so a musket shot pierced him in both thighs. Before the conflict was over, the war would also cost McClung two fingers on his right hand. (The citizens of Columbus, Miss., later gave him a sword engraved with the words he shouted to encourage his men at Monterrey, "Tombigbee Volunteers, follow me!") Despite his bravery, even in the military he was unable to keep his temper in check and according to some sources he quarreled frequently with his superior, a colonel and fellow Kentuckian named Jefferson Davis.

After the war McClung, through some political ties, managed to serve as America's diplomat to Bolivia from 1849 to 1851, but he was sent home after he got into more duels. (Allegedly he killed the British military attaché after the latter made slighting remarks about Americans.) His hopes for a military career were further dashed when his former enemy Jefferson Davis became President Pierce's Secretary of War.

McClung moved back to Jackson, where he gained some reputation as an orator after making a flowery speech to the Mississippi legislature on the death of Henry Clay. He also wrote highly opinionated pieces for newspapers. (In fact, in 1840, McClung had briefly published a virulent Whig newspaper in Jackson called *The True Issue* in which he printed editorials that well reflected his own personality, resulting in yet another duel. As an interesting sidelight, judging from his editorials and

speeches McClung appears to have been very much against the rising secessionist sentiment.)

Overall, however, he was a changed man. Formerly boisterous at least on occasion, he was now always melancholy and sullen. Having failed as a lawyer and deep in debt, it began to dawn on McClung that he was accomplished at little except fighting, and even that questionable pleasure was denied him because he was widely avoided. His war wounds probably caused him considerable lingering physical pain. When depressed, McClung often told friends he wished he had been killed in Mexico.

Statesman and later Confederate General Reuben Davis recalled going to a restaurant in Jackson with Governors Alcorn and Clark, where they saw a drunken and dangerous McClung when he was in the final stages of paranoid dementia. The duelist was eating alone, having scared away all other diners. Davis wrote, "He had a large dueling pistol on either side of a bottle of wine that stood before him, and a bowie knife was disposed between them.... I don't suppose three men ever despatched food with more celerity than we did those unlucky oysters, or with less appreciation of its flavor." McClung belligerently refused to drink with the men, but regaled them with a story about how he had fought off three assassins in that very room earlier in the day. He leaped to his feet and made slashing motions in the air with the knife to demonstrate how he conquered the attackers, barely missing Clark. When McClung returned to his seat he commenced brandishing his hair-trigger pistols. After the patrons finished eating a *very* quick meal, they got up to leave, but McClung, who retained a fondness for Davis, stopped them with a pistol in each hand and demanded to know if Alcorn and Clark believed his story about the three assassins. "Alcorn immediately replied, as blandly as possible, 'Why colonel, do you suppose any gentleman ever questions what you assert?' McClung scowled at him and turned upon Clark, who made the same reply. We were then permitted to depart, which we did with more haste than ceremony."

On a more reflective occasion, his nephew John Henderson McClung visited the duelist in his quarters at the Jackson Hotel after midnight. Despondent, McClung told his nephew that he had trouble sleeping and was "the unhappiest man in America." He exhorted John never to fight a duel. "It took a much braver man to refuse than to fight," he said.

McClung turned increasingly to alcohol for solace and it seemed to some that his own reputation had taken the final toll on his mental faculties. It was whispered that he was haunted by visions of all the men he killed and he had to keep a lamp burning in his room all night, or else he could not sleep.

At last the once flamboyant McClung could no longer bear the burden of the life he had chosen. On the night of Saturday, March 24, 1855, in his lonely room at the Eagle Hotel in Jackson, he wrote the following poem called "Ode to Death:"

> Swiftly speed o'er the waves of time,
> Spirit of death.
> In manhood's home, in youthful prime,
> I woo thy breath.
> For the fading hues of hope have fled,
> Like the Dolphin's light,
> And dark are the clouds above my head
> As the starless night.
> O, vainly the voyager sighs for the rest
> Of the peaceful haven,——
> The pilgrim saint for the home of the blest
> And the calm of heaven;
> The galley slave for the night-wind's breath,
> At burning noon,
> But more gladly I'd spring to thy arms, O death;
> Come soon, come soon!

He pinned the poem to the front of his elegant shirt and blew out his brains with the same dueling pistol he had used to send so many others to the afterlife ahead of him. He was buried in the Coleman family plot, Vicksburg Cemetery.

Willis Westray, Charles Bramble, Laura Irvin, et al.

Eccentric Burials

Most of us, whether we like to admit it or not, are conformists throughout life. A casual glance around any cemetery will convince the viewer that a sense of sameness hounds many persons even after the final curtain falls. One is confronted by rows of nearly identical tombstones bearing the same hackneyed inscriptions: "Not dead but only asleep," "Until we meet again," "Gone but not forgotten." Some modern cemeteries almost resemble Levittowns for the departed.

But there are those who like to be different, even in death. The old-fashioned, unimaginative way to be buried is six feet deep, reclining in a casket. One Kentuckian, Willis P. Westray, had other ideas.

Westray, a farmer from Lowes in (fittingly) Graves County, had a reputation for heavy drinking and general carousing. During one drunken spree, he announced that when he died, he wanted to meet Satan "headlong." Specifically, he wanted to be buried *standing up,* armed with a hatchet and a brickbat, and preferably with a bottle of whiskey as well.

Westray, who had been born on January 6, 1791, died on April 3, 1860, at the age of 69. His survivors followed his instructions, according to a 1937 pamphlet written by students at Lowes High School. A narrow pit was dug in a small cemetery in the forest about a mile east of town. The grave was six feet deep, circular and lined with bricks to keep it from collapsing. Westray was placed in his coffin along with a hatchet. It is not known if the brickbat and whiskey were also included. The coffin was then lowered into the grave in a standing position and covered with the sod.

He still stands under the forest's floor, his marble tombstone leaning upright (like its owner) against a tree. Westray's long-suffering and devout wife, Sarah, is buried beside him. Whether she was interred standing or reclining, and whether Willis' hatchet was useful in fending off Beelzebub, nobody knows.

Westray was not the only Kentuckian who had his own unique notions when it came to burial. Charles Bramble of Cynthiana, Harrison County, was very wealthy, an owner of several farms and worth by one estimate at least $100,000. He was also noted for his omnipresent flask of apple brandy, though he was never known to be intoxicated.

As Bramble got older, his thoughts turned to his eventual demise and the proper means of disposing of his body. He was disturbed by the natural process of decomposition and as he read books about the ancient Egyptian art of embalming, wondered if there were a way to "prove that the idea of dust to dust and ashes to ashes was a back number," as one newspaper account whimsically put it.

A happy thought struck Bramble concerning a way to indefinitely preserve his earthly remains. In 1882, when he was about 65 years old, he had a large sarcophagus hewn out of solid rock at a cost of $900. Then he purchased a barrel of Kentucky bourbon whiskey for embalming purposes. The idea was to have his body dressed in a fine silk outfit and laid out in an iron casket, after which the liquor would be poured over his remains, filling the casket to the brim. This would then be placed in the outer stone sarcophagus, which was made of blue Kentucky limestone. It was more durable than marble, so once the undertakers hermetically sealed the lid and buried the affair in the cold,

cold ground, Bramble would be forever pickled in whiskey. The *Courier-Journal* noted approvingly, "One can but think of the ages to come when this singular coffin shall be unearthed and the remains exposed to the gaze of wondering men. The tombs found recently in Egypt will not be more curious."

(Incidentally, one odd aspect to this already odd story is the grim determination with which the press misrepresented Bramble's name. The *Courier-Journal* and the Louisville *Times* called him Bramlette; the *Richmond Climax*, Bramblette; and the *Lexington Herald*, Bramel.)

Bramble's chance to try out his scheme finally came when he died on January 2, 1897, aged 80 years. His death created great excitement in the community, and on January 5 about 1,500 hardy souls braved the cold to see the unorthodox burial take place at Kentontown Cemetery near Mt. Olivet, Robertson County. It was estimated that it would take a large number of strong horses to drag the two thousand pound coffin to the patiently waiting grave, but the crowd that desired to see Bramble soaked in whiskey and sealed away forever was to be disappointed.

Alas, Bramble had not counted on one thing: between the time his sarcophagus was made and the time of his death, his weight jumped from 160 pounds to 240 pounds. The inner casket would not fit in the limestone sarcophagus. Bramble was placed instead in a noble rosewood casket and "buried like everyone else— in the ground," in the words of the local paper. If only Bramble's plan had succeeded, he would have been a Kentucky native buried in the Kentucky soil inside a Kentucky limestone container and surrounded by Kentucky-made whiskey. That surely would have been a record of some sort.

Unorthodox burials are performed occasionally even in modern times. A couple of examples from Harlan County are cited in *Dark and Bloodied Ground* by Mary Eastman and Mary Bolté. Mrs. Laura Irvin suffered from a lifelong fear of the dark. When she died on March 8, 1961, at age 61, her husband saw to it she would never be without a comforting light. Her casket was placed inside an above-ground mausoleum with a pane of glass in it. At night, a light is kept burning nearby. Visitors to Resthaven Cemetery in Baxter can view her casket inside the crypt through the window, along with floral arrangements left by family members.

According to Eastman and Bolté, an elderly couple in nearby Wallins Creek had to be buried sitting up in their rocking chairs because their bodies were so bent and stiffened with rheumatism.

One grave in Madison County looks perfectly normal— above ground, that is. The two men interred there are not Kentuckians, but their burial was one of the most bizarre in the state's history. On April 11, 1935, a caravan of 41 Roman Catholic gypsies claiming to be Shoshone Indians from Utah, all named Mitchell, were passing near Richmond on their way south. Around 7:30 p.m., the group stopped at the Deatherage service station and camping grounds on U.S. 25, four-and-a-half miles north of town, in search of a campsite. As most of the family stood near the highway discussing their plans, an out-of-control flour truck driven by Lester Smith of Manchester sideswiped three of the six parked cars and hit the rear auto dead on at an estimated 50 miles per hour. A gypsy chieftain, 25-year-old Tom Mitchell, was dead on arrival when his body was taken to Gibson Hospital and

was assumed to have been killed instantly. He left behind a widow and four children. Mitchell's brother Leo, 22, was badly injured and also taken to the hospital. Both were pulled from under the truck; a seven-year-old nephew, Stanley Mitchell, was wounded above the face by flying glass, but recovered.

Most of the gypsies followed the ambulance bearing Tom's body to the hospital. When the clan was informed of Tom's death, they immediately placed lighted candles around the emergency room and began chanting in an unknown tongue. One by one Mitchell's kinsmen entered the morgue where his body was kept and chanted before his corpse. It was nearly an hour before hospital officials persuaded them to leave the building. Town officials housed the nomads in empty city and county jail cells that night, much to the gypsies' displeasure. One other occupant of the county jail that night was the unfortunate Lester Smith, driver of the deadly flour truck, who was detained in a cell far from Mitchell's kinsmen. The next day the gypsies were sent to a nearby camp on the Four Mile road.

Leo Mitchell died of a crushed pelvis, internal injuries and pneumonia on April 13. Other members of the extended family began arriving in Richmond from all over the country, some from as far away as Pittsburgh and New York. The band made arrangements with Andrew "Jack" Turpin, proprietor of a local funeral home, to have the two brothers buried in the potter's field section of Richmond Cemetery. In an interview with *Courier-Journal* columnist Byron Crawford in 1985, Turpin recalled, "They wanted a certain type casket, and I said, 'Where's the money coming from?' They said, 'There will be a man come in from New York with big money.' He did. He finally came with big money and paid off everything." However, Turpin also caught the gypsies making long distance calls to relatives all over the world and charging them to his funeral home.

About 1,000 local curiosity seekers, as well as 125 members of the Mitchells' tribe, were present at the brothers' visitation at the funeral home. The service in the cemetery took place on April 15, and was attended by a throng of 2,000. At the request of the Mitchells, Father O.L. Poole of St. Mark's Catholic Church blessed the grave. After the priest departed, the funeral was officiated by a gypsy preacher who quoted the Gospel in English, but also spoke in a strange tongue. Stranger still, the brothers were buried according to their custom: the Mitchells wore their hats and shoes, and each casket was filled with shaving soap, towels, a razor, a mirror, a comb and cigarettes. Their fellow tribesmen stuffed the pockets of the dead men with "a right smart money in half dollars and quarters," as Turpin recalled. It was felt the Mitchells might need these items in the afterlife.

After the caskets were lowered into the double grave, the members of the tribe lined up under the tent and each threw a handful of dirt down onto the lids. When the caskets were covered, the gypsies opened a bottle of sweet wine and poured its contents on the grave.

About a week after the accident, the relatives drove away for parts unknown. But they forgot neither the Mitchell brothers nor the town where they were laid to rest. For many years after the burial, bands of gypsies would sporadically return to the plot in Richmond Cemetery, where they performed ceremonial dances and other rituals at the grave. Cemetery superintendent Clarence Hensley related in 1985 that the gypsies visited the Mitchells' grave four times between 1972 and 1977:

"Sometimes there'll be one car, and sometimes there'll be three carloads of people. They'll light a cigarette for themselves; they'll light one for Tom, they'll light one for Leo and stick it up in the ground. They get the best of champagne and the best of beer; they'll take a drink, and they'll pour a little out on each grave. They'll get up on that rock and jump off and turn somersaults. They'll dance a jig, and that girl will holler that she's dancing with Tom, or she's dancing with Leo. You can't but help be a little leery of it, the way they carry on." During one visit, the tribe arrived in a new Cadillac and left without paying for services rendered after superintendent Hensley cleaned the tombstone.

The brothers still sleep in Richmond Cemetery amidst their towels, razors, bars of soap, and their collection of small change. Grave robbers have tried to unearth their caskets several times in the past, but always cease their activities just before reaching pay dirt. Perhaps the wanderers also buried a good old-fashioned gypsy curse along with the Mitchells' store of earthly possessions.

Leonard "Live-Forever" Jones

Lunatic

One of Kentucky's most charming eccentrics could be found almost daily in the hotel later renamed the Willard, located directly across from the Jefferson County court house in the days just before the Civil War. The old fellow was always poorly dressed, unshaven, and had a wild mane of white, shoulder-length hair, but he was good company. He did not live in the hotel; he simply loitered on the porch or in the lobby, talking to anyone who would listen. He rarely lacked an audience, because his conversation was entertaining enough. The local press commented on his excellent memory, his knowledge of Scripture and his dry wit. He would discuss nearly any topic in a sensible and sane manner, but almost always, his favorite subject would come up, either naturally or because he found a creative way to shoehorn it into the discussion. And when he really warmed up, all eyes would turn to him and all other conversation stopped. Inevitably he would be surrounded by a sea of faces, some blank and dumbfounded, some smiling, some barely able to suppress grins. Sober and earnest, completely unaware of how he seemed to others, the man would tell people he had figured out the secret of immortality. He was never going to die.

Leonard Jones was his name. It was one of many names. At various times he was also called eccentric, crazy, the Mendicant Madman of Louisville and "the most extraordinary character of his time." But the name that really stuck was "Live-Forever" Jones. He was born in Frankfort, Va., on July 3, 1797, and his family moved to Henderson (now Union) County, Ky., when he was seven years old.

Jones as a young man was a land speculator and amassed considerable property. The *Louisville Daily Democrat* later described him as having been "a man of great originality and power, and in earlier days gave promise of a noble manhood." He planned to marry a young woman of central Kentucky, but she broke off the engagement. Devastated, Jones' mental state declined.

One possible symptom of his increasing derangement is that he changed his religion as often as other men change their hats. He started out as a member of the United Brethren, then became a Methodist. After that he joined the Shakers at Pleasant Hill in Mercer County. While there he fell in love with a Shaker woman named Sister Nancy, former wife of Brother John. He entered a fast of 40 days' duration, refusing to eat "till Sister Nancy would feed him with her hands." She finally broke down and prepared a meal, which Jones ate from a table.

Much to his chagrin, he realized he had broken his solemn oath: he had eaten from a *table,* not from Sister Nancy's hands! To remedy this, he began another fast. This time around, the Shaker temptress flatly refused to feed him, even if he should starve to death. Jones sadly gave up his second fast, only to see John and Nancy re-marry. This latest disappointment in love was too much to bear, and Jones left the Shakers.

Before long he was baptized by a Mormon preacher, but he quickly gave up that religion when he found he could not speak in tongues as promised. Jones' next religion *du jour* was Quakerism. He soon had a falling out with them as well, and was left in need of a spiritual anchor.

The anchor showed up around 1835 in the form of a bizarre itinerant minister named McDaniel, who preached the doctrine that if a man lived right, fasted frequently and had sufficient faith, he would never have to die and could be immortal right here on earth. It was just the message the unstable Jones wanted to hear. Taken with the idea, he joined the minister and the pair traveled through the state preaching the live-forever doctrine to anyone who would listen.

The two had ambitious plans to build a city on the site of what is presently the town of Columbus in Hickman County for their expected throngs of live-forever disciples. It was to be a village "where death, coffins, and graveyards were to be unknown." The question remained to be settled, however, whether McDaniel or Jones would have the supreme ruling position in the new city. The pair engaged in a two-hour staring contest to determine the answer, but it ended in a draw.

Their next step was to win some converts to their two-man religion. Eventually the elderly McDaniel took ill while proselytizing in Ohio and, regardless of the sincerity of his belief, he died just like everyone else. That spelled an end to their dream of a Utopian city. One might expect Jones to have found another religion after this setback, but his conviction that he was immortal remained unshaken. (When someone asked Jones if McDaniel's demise had shaken his faith, he admitted, "No, but I was very much embarrassed to preach at his funeral!")

He attended every church in Louisville, always sitting in the front row, often interrupting the sermon with his own comments. Rare was the religious leader visiting town who did not become acquainted with Live-Forever Jones.

Louisville's most prominent lunatic had another major obsession besides religion, and that was politics. He was convinced that as a representative of God on earth, he ought to hold some public office, whether state or federal, in order to reform corrupt politics. Consequently he formed his own party, the "High Moral" ticket, of which he was both head and the only member. It was his belief that all elected officials should be partisans of his new faction. He proceeded to become one of the greatest political pests the country has ever witnessed by perpetually running for vacant offices at election time. He ran for Congress in the Paducah district several years consecutively, never winning. Then he stumped in other districts as well, but if he ever received any votes history has failed to record the fact. At one point he considered trying to become a Massachusetts senator.

Jones had no qualms about harassing with lawsuits his rivals who did get elected, on the grounds that he should have won their offices. He made frequent trips to Washington to annoy legislators, against whom he constantly filed suit in chancery court. In 1867 Live-Forever declared himself the rightful governor of Kentucky. He considered his claim proven after the untimely death on September 8 of the elected governor, John Larue Helm, just five days into his second term.

The *Louisville Courier* dryly remarked of the monomaniac's obsession with politics: "No political meeting ever passed off within a hundred miles of Louisville that did not hear from Live-Forever Jones. Though a warm sympathizer with the South, he believed himself the only man who could save the country, and though his speech was usually the last, it was always there." A reporter from the *Louisville Daily Democrat* added: "We have heard him and seen him often, a wreck and a ruin, and a sad burlesque and commentary on politics and political life. Yet at times the strange old man startled his hearers with strong gleams of reason, and through it all not one man ever heard a wicked or profane or vulgar word from his tongue." Jones' mannerisms while speechifying were certainly attention-getting, if nothing else. He was prone to jump up and down for minutes at a time and strike his hickory cane against a table to emphasize his points, sometimes so loudly that he drowned out his own oratory. Live-Forever was always at a loss to understand why the newspapers never printed his speeches and why other preachers ignored his "High Moral" party.

For 20 years running Live-Forever declared himself a candidate for the presidency. In the 1856 election, when his name did not turn up on the ballots, Jones declared the election illegal and sought a written injunction against the winner, James Buchanan. He also failed to win this highest of offices in 1860. Live-Forever retaliated in both cases by filing lawsuits against Buchanan and Lincoln, but the state's legislators, who had no intention of ever hearing the cases, always made certain the suits were moved to the end of the docket and thus were always to be heard in the next session. Nevertheless, Jones felt justice was served in his cause when Lincoln was assassinated in 1865. He interpreted the act as divine punishment for the country's failure to give "the morally elected candidate" the presidency.

That Live-Forever was a very moral person nobody had any doubt. He had no discernible vices, and neither drank nor swore. He was fastidious about paying off any debts he incurred. However, his

penchant for fasting caused him trouble. "Occasionally extreme hunger would carry him beyond his doctrine, but he would never eat in the presence of anyone, and when discovered would denounce the food as 'moral poison'.... When pressed by hunger he would borrow from a friend, but this was the last thing he would do, sometimes suffering excruciatingly before he would ask," said the *Courier*. The *Daily Democrat* offered similar praise: "A disordered mind might lead him into follies, but even among his rags and squalor, his tangled locks and patriarchal beard, he stood with heart so pure that he rebuked his mockers."

Live-Forever's highly developed sense of morality also created occasional social problems. He haunted the local police court, and if he felt an injustice was being done to a prisoner he would disrupt the proceedings and loudly denounce the judge and lawyers. Sometimes he would offer to act as attorney for the accused. He was usually thrown in jail for contempt, but invariably was released after a few hours. Jones practiced the high moral standards he preached. An admiring reporter once wrote that "Honest, truthful, generous, and candid, he was no mean imitation of the Son of Man." Yet for all his sincerity, Jones apparently never won a single convert to his faith.

Perhaps the most touching aspect in the story of Live-Forever Jones is that the city of Louisville adopted him as an informal favorite son. Despite his eccentric beliefs, he was gently humored by nearly everyone. Politicians would pretend to file the crazy ballots he handed them. Whenever he made a speech, the crowd would applaud and cheer as if he were Henry Clay returned from the grave. A reporter commented, "We do not recollect of any indignity ever being offered him at public meetings." Though he could have passed as a hobo in appearance, Jones was acquainted with almost every prominent family in the state. No one ever suggested he be sent to an asylum. Generous citizens gave him money and clothes for his comfort, but Live-Forever would always donate his bounty, in a most Christian way, to those less fortunate than himself. The *Courier* recalled "He gave away as fast as he received. You might give him a dollar or five dollars at the post office, and before he would go a square he would give it all away if he happened to meet with objects which he deemed more needy than himself." On one occasion, friends from Paducah gave him a horse, complete with bridle and saddle, so he could ride when preaching and spreading the live-forever gospel. Somewhere between Paducah and Mayfield, Jones gave the horse and accessories to a barefoot beggar.

William Carnes Kendrick, writing in 1937, distinctly remembered seeing Jones in Louisville while a small boy. "When we youngsters were in that locality [of the hotel]— really we would make it convenient to go by often— we would always stop with open eyes and gapping [sic] mouths, stand staring at this curiosity of a man, who said he was going to live forever, and we had no more sense than to believe him."

Years of exposure and intentionally starving himself inevitably resulted in Live-Forever's catching a bad case of pneumonia. As usual, he refused to ask friends for help. He was finally taken to the Louisville Hospital, but by then it was obvious to everyone except himself that the end was near. He refused to take any food or medicine, declaring his sickness was moral, not physical, and that even if he were ill it could not result in his death. Jones would not even permit attendants to remove his shoes.

Though one must admire his steely confidence in his beliefs,

Jones did indeed depart this world peacefully on the morning of August 30, 1868, aged 71. The *Daily Democrat* eulogized the town lunatic, saying Jones was a "ridiculous orator, the jest of the mob and the multitude, and yet there can be written on his tomb: He lived and died a gentleman... He was a weak but good old man." The *Daily Courier* put an eloquent obituary on the front page on September 1, remarking that "his name [was] familiar in every household in Kentucky," and ran a lengthy story about Jones on September 12. Even Collins' revised *History of Kentucky* found it worthwhile to mention the death of Live-Forever Jones, only with an erroneous date of death. Jones would have thought *any* date of death a mistake.

Simon Kracht

Resurrectionist

It is not now difficult for medical students to find human corpses to dissect for anatomical study. Many generous persons are willing to donate their bodies to science. Until recently, preserved human body parts could easily be purchased from medical school supply catalogs. Computer software can now provide students with a "virtual body" they may dissect and explore with aplomb.

This was not always the case. For centuries, the dissection of human cadavers, even for beneficial medical study, was frowned upon and practitioners risked severe penalties. Practically the only bodies that legally could be examined were those of hanged criminals; the knowledge that they were to be dissected after death was held to be part of the criminal's punishment.

Yet a medical student who does not have a real human body to examine is like a beginning swimmer who stays out of the water. The thirst for knowledge could sometimes be quenched with a quick trip to a fresh grave in the cemetery. Well into the 19th century there was a seedy underground business by "resurrectionists," men who would dig up the bodies of the recently deceased and supply them to medical schools for a fee, no questions asked. On occasion medical students themselves would raid graveyards at night, armed with shovels, lanterns, large bags, and a surfeit of courage.

Offbeat Kentuckians

Simon Kracht, resurrectionist for the University of Louisville's Medical School, with the tools of his trade. The handwritten caption reads: "Died by his own hand Nov. 13, 1875—Simon Kracht— Resurrector."

Courtesy Kornhauser Health Sciences Library, University of Louisville, Louisville, Ky.

The University of Louisville's medical school had an employee in the 1870s who functioned nominally as a janitor, but had another duty, as well. He was a German immigrant named Simon Kracht, formerly a minister, and he surreptitiously kept the school well stocked with bodies. According to his obituary in the *Louisville Ledger*, Kracht had worked for the medical school since about 1863.

A 1984 dissertation by Dwayne Cox, "A History of the University of Louisville," notes that many bodies dissected by students in the 19th century "came from the lower rungs of the city's social and economic ladder, especially slaves and free blacks." The *Ledger* claimed that "half the Negroes in the neighborhood of Ninth and Chestnut believed with fear and trembling that they would 'go to [Simon Kracht] after death.'" Should the supply of poverty-stricken corpses be low, however, Kracht had other methods. An alumnus who later became president of the American Medical Association, John Allan Wyeth (class of 1869), remembered in his autobiography *With Sabre and Scalpel:* "The activity of the dissecting-room janitor kept us in a sufficient quantity of cadavers...we did not know [how he got some of the bodies], and it probably was just as well that no inquiry was instituted."

Wyeth also wrote that Kracht was "the rock upon which our anatomical church was founded, and to whom it was said the keys of Cave Hill Cemetery had been given." It seems unlikely the sextons of Cave Hill, an upper-crust cemetery, would give the janitor *carte blanche* to raid their grounds. However, according to *Courier-Journal* columnist Jim Adams, it has been theorized that part of the $10 fee each student paid to take an anatomy course was used to bribe cemetery officials. Wyeth's words certainly seem to imply as much. In addition to procuring bodies for the school, Kracht had the equally unpleasant duty of disposing of the remains after the students had finished their studies. This chore consisted of tossing the flesh and other refuse "in an immensely deep dry well," Cox writes, and presumably adding a necessary dash of acid or quicklime to keep down the fragrance.

By the early 1870s Kracht's side job was considered of such importance to the school that his likeness was included in an album of 44 photographs featuring the medical faculty. Though Kracht was officially only a janitor, the picture has a handwritten notation,

"Resurrector." The albumen print photo shows Kracht looking every inch the ghoul. He is posing rather brazenly with a shovel in one hand and, across his shoulders, a sack from which a human skull protrudes. The *Ledger* described him thusly: "Dickens could have written an entire new book about him, had these two gentlemen been contemporaries and acquaintances.... In his make-up he was the very man to adorn the novelist's page— low, puffy, blear-eyed, peculiar. He was never known to wear a coat [although he is wearing one in the photo], whatever might be the range of the mercury, and his upper person was only protected from the vulgar gaze of humanity by a thick woolen shirt of a leaden hue, which he wore in both winter and summer." The reporter added with the breezy sexism of those times that "If [Kracht's shirt] did look like it had never been washed, that was of course his wife's fault."

Kracht was immensely popular with both the faculty and the medical students, who called him "Old Simon." The students were aware that his contributions made their education possible. Possibly they were also relieved someone else was willing to do the dirty work.

But the life of a resurrectionist isn't all fun and pleasure. Kracht's first wife died while relatively young. The record does not state whether he dutifully toted her to the dissecting table. Kracht married again, but his home life was not exemplary. He and his second wife quarreled frequently. In 1873 Kracht's brother in St. Louis shuffled off this mortal coil, allegedly as a suicide. Even worse, Kracht himself nearly died in Spring 1874 when his stepdaughter made soup "out of the refuse barrel of the college," which contained all sorts of discarded drugs, poisons, and other nameless horrors. The family unwittingly partook of the unappetizing meal, and two hours later everyone in the house was violently ill. The *Ledger* reporter recalled, "The writer saw them when they were writhing in their agony— the janitor, his wife, her daughter and two sons occupied different places on the floor of their room. But they were saved from death through the kindly, or unkindly, interposition of medical aid."

The slowly recovering Kracht's mental state was not helped by the financial hardships placed upon him by his second wife. Sometime in 1874 Mrs. Kracht took about $1,000 of the janitor's *very* hard-earned savings without his knowledge and loaned it to her brother, who promptly spent it all and went bankrupt. Outraged, Kracht sued his brother-in-law to regain his money, vowing that if he lost the suit he would commit suicide. Soon afterwards, Mrs. Kracht deserted her husband, but not before helping herself to an additional $1,500 of his money. She gradually returned with only a fraction of the sum, but Kracht welcomed her back. Spurred by his financial woes and marital problems, Kracht fell deeply into bouts of drinking and depression.

On the morning of November 12, 1875, Kracht had a bitter argument with his wife in their quarters at the university. Despondent, he went to work. At about two in the afternoon he opened a medicinal bottle of morphine and swallowed 22 grains of the drug. He then approached several students and instructed them to give his building keys to the faculty since he had just taken poison and was not long for the world. The students assumed he was joking and went about their business. Their reaction may seem callous, but Kracht had long been in the strange habit of scaring bystanders by pretending to ingest poison. The medical students thought he was crying wolf again.

Not long afterward, an alarmed Mrs. Kracht ran into the courtyard and told some students her husband was seriously ill. The budding

physicians tended to Kracht, giving him some emetics that proved useless. Doctors Cowling, Bodine and Roberts watched over their beloved janitor and body snatcher constantly. A contemporary news account relates that Professor Holland "tried electricity to keep [Kracht] awake." One wonders what exactly that process entailed. The resurrectionist rallied briefly, and at one point he arose and asked if someone would help him walk in the yard outside. Two of the students in attendance helped him to his feet, but after walking barely 10 steps from the house Kracht fainted and remained comatose until he died a few minutes after one in the morning of November 13, nearly 12 hours after swallowing the morphine. He was fifty-three years old.

Kracht's funeral took place on November 14 in the medical building, a highly unusual occurrence that illustrates how well-liked he was by his employers. The *Courier-Journal* ran an obituary on November 15 that seems ripe with dark humor if one reads between the lines: "In his humble way Simon was a faithful servant of medical science, and the tribute of respect and appreciation which was paid his remains yesterday was eminently appropriate. It will be difficult for the faculty to find one who can fill his place."

Kracht was buried in Grave 6, Range 42, Section M, of Cave Hill Cemetery, the very hunting grounds he allegedly plundered while on the job. In 1992 columnist Jim Adams wrote: "Standing alone here at his grave, I found it fun to wonder whether Simon's successor ever came to retrieve him. Whether his flesh and refuse might really be in a deep dry well at Eighth and Chestnut. Especially considering that Simon had the audacity to commit suicide at midterm. But there's no evidence of disturbance; the earth is packed and even slightly rounded below his now-worn headstone."

But Adams also noted that the grave beside Kracht's suspiciously bore "a rather soft indentation."

Phil Arnold

Diamond Mine Swindler

The history of crime teems with uncreative, humdrum felonies: copycat murders, cut-and-dried kidnappings, by-the-book swindles. But in the early 1870s a Kentucky native out west masterminded a cheat that has yet to be duplicated. In the words of the *New Yorker,* Phil Arnold was "The first and, as far as history records, the last American to salt a diamond mine.... An ordinary prospector merely tries to find deposits of precious minerals; a creative prospector places them in the ground for others to find."

The story begins in February 1872, when Arnold, a Civil War veteran and native of Elizabethtown, Hardin County, walked into the Bank of California in San Francisco. He was accompanied by a cousin, John Slack of Howe Valley, Ky. They had spent some time in the western states as prospectors, and in fact, several years prior sold a claim of theirs at Marysville, Ca., for $50,000.

As they approached the teller, Arnold carried a small leather pouch. Arnold asked if the bank would deposit the bag for safekeeping. The teller asked to see the contents so he could write a receipt. Arnold and Slack opened the pouch and revealed a handful of unpolished, uncut diamonds with a few rubies and garnets, as well. After getting their receipt, the cousins left the establishment.

The amazed teller rushed to tell the bank president, William C.

Ralston, what he had just seen. Ralston assumed the duo must have found a diamond mine and immediately sent representatives of the bank to find Arnold and Slack and urge them to return for a business discussion.

Once the prospectors were back in the president's office, he asked where they found the jewels. The pair claimed they had discovered a fabulous mine in Arizona, which happened to be dangerously located in Apache territory. Ralston informed them that he knew a group of financiers who would buy the mine from them, for a fair price, of course. Arnold and Slack seemed interested and offered to take an expert of the bank's choice to see the mine— but only if the man would remain blindfolded while traveling to and from the mine. The bank agreed to this rather suspicious condition, no doubt believing the prospectors' only motive was the desire to keep the mine's exact location a secret.

The financiers chose their diamond expert, a miner named General David Colton, who boarded a Union Pacific train with Arnold and Slack. The journey took them from San Francisco to Butte, Mont. They explained to Colton, who had been told the mine was in Arizona, that it was actually in Colorado; they had stated it was in Arizona merely to throw claim jumpers off the trail. Once arrived, the agent was blindfolded and rode with the prospectors in the desert for four days. At last, they reached a high mesa in Jackson County, Co., eight miles below the Wyoming border, and the cousins removed the blindfold.

Colton was urged to examine the edge of a rock in the mesa. (Some accounts state that he was asked to dig in an anthill.) Obediently, he scooped his hands repeatedly under the edge. At first he received nothing but handfuls of sand. Then all at once he pulled out two uncut diamonds, followed by four more in the next handful. The cousins told him to select two for examination. After he placed two diamonds in his pocket, Colton was again blindfolded and the trio returned to San Francisco.

The diamonds were examined by the famous jewelers, Sloan's. Then they were sent to Tiffany's in New York for a second opinion. Both organizations declared the diamonds authentic; Tiffany, in fact, personally estimated the diamonds were worth $150,000. He unwittingly overstated their value. Arnold cleverly counted on the fact that most professional jewelers deal with already-cut diamonds and have little experience with estimating the value of uncut gems.

The promoters insisted on sending someone else to see the secret mine. General Colton had been a gold miner, but the financiers wanted to send Henry Janin, who was an actual mining engineer. His reputation held that he had examined over 600 mines in his career without making a single mistake. If anyone would be difficult to fool, it should have been Janin. This time Arnold was taking a serious risk, but he readily agreed to show the salted mine to the second expert. Janin accompanied the two prospectors blindfolded to the mine, and came away with the same exciting results: the mesa was full of real diamonds and rubies, and a seemingly limitless supply of them! They were practically there for the taking! Janin estimated the 3,000-acre mesa could be worth $5 million per acre, and if the surrounding land were just as rich in minerals, it could be worth billions.

Ralston and his financiers were ecstatic, but they said nothing about the mine's potential value to Arnold and Slack. The bankers hoped to buy the mine at a fraction of its real worth. Quietly, $10 million was spent to create the San Francisco and New York Mining and Commercial Company with 100,000 shares of stock— none offered for sale to the public.

But the secret did not stay secret for long. Suddenly 25 separate mining companies were on the prowl in the region where the mine was supposedly located, each determined to find it first. Ralston could wait no longer. He offered to buy the mine from the cousins for $600,000, a large sum to be sure, but a pittance when one considers that the mine was estimated to be worth up to, and beyond, $200 million. Arnold and Slack feigned outrage at the low payment, then accepted it and hurried back home to Kentucky, leaving Ralston and company delighted at the ease with which they had skinned the country bumpkins.

However, soon it became evident that there was plenty of cheating to go around. Before Ralston's firm could start digging, another company deduced the location of the mesa and beat them to it. And this company found, after much digging, that there were no naturally formed diamonds in the mesa at all. The only ones ever found were the

Offbeat Kentuckians

ones the cousins intended the experts to find. Arnold and Slack had, in fact, cheated Ralston and his financiers. A young government geologist, Clarence King, surveyed the mesa and found a few stray diamonds planted in geologic locations where they could never have been placed by nature. Some had clearly been stomped shallowly into the ground by foot; others were found placed between crevices in rocks, and under a magnifying glass the rocks were seen to bear tool marks. One gem was found in a hollow tree stump.

Also, King pointed out, the mesa supposedly yielded four different kinds of diamonds, and also rubies, garnets, spinels, sapphires, emeralds and amethysts, "an association of minerals impossible of occurrence in nature." The clincher was when King's assistant found a cut diamond in the ground. It had accidentally been mixed in with the uncut gems, and neither Arnold nor Slack noticed.

A British investor finally revealed that in 1871, the cousins went to Amsterdam and London and purchased about $35,000 worth of raw South African diamonds. They put some in the leather pouch as bait, and the others they planted in the mesa in Colorado. Soon after these revelations, the humiliated bank president Ralston paid off his investors in full. However, this financial strain plus the Panic of 1873 rendered his bank insolvent, and in 1875 he committed suicide by drowning in San Francisco Bay.

Most of the investors in the fraudulent diamond mine were too embarrassed to file suits against their swindlers. But one of the greedier victims, William Lent, was not about to take getting cheated lightly. He sued Arnold, but Kentucky refused to extradite the culprit to California. Lent then traveled to Kentucky and filed a civil suit in Louisville, but whenever his process servers went to Elizabethtown to serve an attachment on Arnold, they were met by protective citizens who icily insisted Arnold was not in the county at present. He was considered something of a hometown hero. (Arnold was born on November 5, 1829, in Hardin County — the same county, it has been pointed out, that gave the world Abraham Lincoln.) After much legal wrangling, Phil Arnold agreed to compromise by paying $150,000, half of his share from the sale, for immunity from further litigation.

Arnold was still left with a fortune, and he used it to purchase

500 acres of farmland and open a store. However, his pride and joy was his magnificent $18,000 two-story brick house with its 34-acre yard. It featured enormous hallways, marble fireplaces, 12-foot ceilings and a brass chandelier. Rumor had it Arnold's mansion contained a safe with a half million dollars worth of cash in it, and that the house had secret tunnels in the basement.

Ironically, Arnold became a banker himself. Presumably his own experience taught him to meet any diamond miners who may have entered his establishment with a jaundiced eye.

It came to pass that Arnold got into a business disagreement with a rival banker named Harry N. Holdsworth. On August 15, 1878, Arnold spent considerable time drinking and brooding at Lott's Saloon. In walked Holdsworth. Arnold knocked his rival to the floor and pounded him with both fists. Finally, he let Holdsworth go, but the latter returned shortly with a sawed-off shotgun. Arnold was supremely confident because he was armed with an expensive ornamental revolver,

72

while his rival had only a cheap weapon. However, the added expense did Arnold no good. Holdsworth was a better shot, or was simply more sober, and Arnold ended up severely wounded. He died of pneumonia in his fine home on February 8, 1879.

Most sources claim Arnold's cousin and partner in crime, John Slack, vanished and was never heard from again. Some writers have even theorized that he was murdered by persons unknown after receiving his share of the money. However, in 1967 author Bruce Woodard determined that Slack had moved to St. Louis, where he made coffins and caskets for the firm of Wilson, Warner and Company. In September 1874, Slack ambitiously became president of the St. Louis Coffin and Manufacturing Company. The business failed, after which the former miner moved to White Oaks, N. M., where he lived off his fortune and continued working as a casket maker. According to columnist Jim Bishop, Slack rarely discussed his part in the great swindle, but he remained nettled by the financiers' eagerness to cheat two Kentucky prospectors. "Now tell me, which group were the thieves?" he would ask his listeners. Slack died on July 26, 1896, at the age of seventy-six, much respected by the town.

Arnold's mansion remains in Elizabethtown, where it is currently being used as a halfway house. It has developed a local reputation for being haunted, complete with muffled voices and dragging chains. The author spoke with Richmond resident Barbara McMahon, whose mother was born in the house in 1911, when it was still being used as a private residence and who lived there throughout her childhood. McMahon's mother later wrote a series of short stories about growing up in Phil Arnold's house. She recalled neighborhood children digging up the yard in search of diamonds. They had about as much luck as Arnold's original investors.

Honest Dick Tate

Absconder

How inaccurate can a person's nickname be? You might get a profane answer if you could ask the voters who elected James William "Honest Dick" Tate, Kentucky's State Treasurer from 1867 to 1888. Oddly enough, the vast majority of books on Kentucky history have little if anything to say about the brazen thievery of Tate, even though his perfidy had a direct and durable effect on state politics.

He was someone whose background suggested he could be trusted. Tate was born in Franklin County on January 2, 1831, to parents who were of solid Kentucky stock. His father was a farmer and his mother a preacher's daughter. His paternal grandfather was a Revolutionary War soldier. Starting when he was only 17, Tate worked as a respectable post office clerk in Frankfort for several years. He entered politics by becoming an assistant secretary of state from 1854-55 and 1859-63. From 1865 to 1867 he was also assistant clerk in the state's House of Representatives. In 1867 he decided to run for the office of state treasurer. His reputation for honesty was so great that he not only won, he kept getting re-elected every two years until he had held the post over two decades.

By 1878 he was prominent enough to be featured in the prestigious *Biographical Encyclopaedia of Kentucky*. The book tells us Tate "materially contributed, by his personal popularity, to the great success of the [Democratic] Party" in the 1867 election. It continues, "Biennially, since that time, without opposition in his own party, he has been successively re-elected by popular majorities, perhaps exceeding those obtained by any other candidate for office in the State. From these evidences of popularity, it would seem that his lease on the office might be regarded as a fixed fact..."

In addition to being popular with his fellow legislators, the capsule biography describes Tate as "upright in his dealings," "universally esteemed," and refers to him as a treasurer whose "judgment is held in high esteem and his integrity, prudence, and foresight are regarded of

State treasurer James W. Tate, formerly known as "Honest Dick." From the Louisville *Courier-Journal* of March 21, 1888. *Courtesy Courier-Journal.*

the highest order." These glowing praises would seem cruelly ironic 10 years later. The volume also features an engraving of Tate, then 47 years old. With his melancholy eyes, receding hairline and walrus mustache, he looks trustworthy indeed, rather like a Sunday school superintendent.

Tate's career as treasurer was unblemished until 1888. In retrospect, there were warning signs galore. For several weeks in a row, Tate deposited only checks— not cash— in the state's account at the bank. In addition, Tate suddenly paid several of his outstanding personal debts. Then on March 14, one of Tate's clerks, Henry Murray, saw him in his office filling two tobacco sacks with gold and silver coins. He also bundled a considerable amount of paper money. It would later be estimated that altogether he left his office with about $100,000, worth over $1 million in today's currency. Tate left behind a note saying he would return to Frankfort on March 16, then departed for Louisville. Nobody found this in any way unusual. After all, Tate's office required him to handle large sums of money, and besides, he had an untarnished reputation for honesty.

Honest Dick lingered at the Louisville Hotel with all that cash for a couple of days, at one point leaving to attend a show at Macauley's Theatre. Then he boarded a train bound for Cincinnati and vanished, leaving behind his wife Lucy and their grown daughter, Edmoina.

Such was Tate's spotless standing in the eyes of his peers that no one was worried even after a day or two without word from the absent treasurer. Then several more days passed. The collective brow of the legislature began to perspire. Finally, nearly a week after Tate left his office with so much money, officials faced the hard truth: Tate was not coming back, and he had taken a substantial amount of the state's treasury with him. The embezzlement was revealed in the press on March 20, and soon afterward the General Assembly offered a reward of $5,000 for information leading to the arrest of Tate.

Tate was by no means the first embezzler the voters of Kentucky had elected to a high office. In the 1840s, State Treasurer Colonel James Davidson defaulted to the tune of $80,000; Thomas Page defalcated while State Auditor in the 1850s; and as recently as 1876, the treasurer of Covington had robbed the city coffers of $57,000. But none of these

Offbeat Kentuckians

previous scandals evoked quite the excitement of Tate's misappropria-tion, probably because the amount he stole was astronomical in com-parison. The public was infuriated by his audacious crime, and one con-temporary declared that nothing had created such a stir in Kentucky since the Civil War. The sense of general astonishment was well expressed in a pained *Louisville Courier-Journal* editorial: "The fall of a man like Tate is a grave public calamity. His betrayal of his trust is a shock to one's faith in one's fellow-man. What his temptations have been no man can know, but his crime is unpardonable. He has wronged a people who have trusted him implicitly; he has betrayed a party which, for twenty years, has delighted to honor him."

When it was realized Tate was gone for good, his financial records were immediately examined. They were so haphazardly kept, probably intentionally, that a squad of accountants had to labor 10 days to sort everything out. They found Kentucky's treasury was short a lit-tle over $247,000, of which $100,000 had been personally carried away by the treasurer. They also discovered that Tate had put some of the missing money to personal use; he bought coal mines and land in other states, thus using his official rank to enrich himself. He also gambled in "wildcat" stocks using state money. Tate had been filching small sums here and there since at least 1872, and in all that time no one had ever troubled to double check his records. If you couldn't trust Honest Dick Tate, who could you trust?

More bitter revelations were to come. Some state politicians turned out to have had a vested interest in making sure no one exam-ined Tate's records too closely. Certain officials, including judges, had been in the habit of going to Tate whenever they needed a little quick cash or an advance on their salaries, and he was only too happy to loan them money right out of the treasury's funds. This, of course, was ille-gal. The committee found signed notes for sums ranging from a paltry $1.85 to a breathtaking $5,340. Tate even gave Governor Leslie an advance of several dollars on his salary in July 1872. Some officials had already paid back their loans, while many others had not. But all who accepted Tate's ingratiating offer were caught with their hands in the till. It was additionally found that Tate had committed for-gery and doctored bank deposit statements to mask any discrepancies.

Not all of the missing money had been stolen or illegally loaned; some of it was simply lost due to Tate's bookkeeping eccentricities. As historians Hambleton Tapp and James C. Klotter noted, "There seemed to be no distinction in his operations between public and private funds." Tate was apt to treat a huge sum of cash as casually as if it were loose change to hide under the mattress. He had been in the habit of simply keeping some state money in bags around the office instead of depositing it in banks where it belonged. A thousand dollars was found under a safe, where it had fallen out, been pushed under and then long forgotten.

Republicans made political hay out of Tate's departure, prompting the *Courier-Journal,* a Democratic paper, to remark with some heat: "Did the Republican party ever turn out of the fold one of its black sheep with half the promptness with which the Democrats of the General Assembly have expedited the dismissal of the late Treasurer of Kentucky? If that party has ever done so well we should be pleased to see a bill of particulars setting forth the fact. We turn the rascals out."

Tate had been able to get away with his misdeeds for so long largely due to the laziness or duplicity of many fellow politicians. By turns outraged and embarrassed, the Kentucky House of

Representatives impeached Tate *in absentia* and the Senate officially found him guilty and removed him from office on March 30. It was, as of this writing, the last impeachment of a public official in Kentucky history. During the hearings, Governor Buckner testified that he had been planning to have Tate's financial records undergo a routine examination by a committee. The knowledge that he was at long last about to be exposed was probably the motive for Tate's sudden flight.

Despite it all, Tate still had supporters. As one of his friends, Colonel Oliver Lucas, told the *Courier-Journal*, "I shall always feel that much of [the money] went, in the shape of loans, to the men who will now be only too ready to kick him after he is down." Some of Tate's associates felt he was, in fact, a victim, and his only serious flaw was being too generous with friends who were eager to dip into the state's funds by taking advantage of the treasurer's kind nature. Their belief was that when Tate realized investigators were about to discover an improper financial discrepancy he could not explain away, he simply fled the state to avoid facing the damage done to his good name. The problem with this theory is that it does not explain why Tate felt he should carry away $100,000 of the state's cash in his flight from disgrace.

But where did Honest Dick Tate flee? At the time, Tate's family claimed to have heard no word from him and said they believed he committed suicide. In 1897, his daughter, Mrs. Edmoina Martin, filed suit in the Franklin Circuit Court to collect on a $5,000 insurance policy Tate had taken out on himself in 1883. She argued that since he had not contacted his family in over seven years, he should be presumed legally dead. She admitted that from April to December 1888 she secretly received at least four letters from her father. They were postmarked Canada (British Columbia), then Japan and China, then finally San Francisco. (In the last letter Tate complained of having a bad cold and wrote that he hoped to come home.) A man named Will Jett testified that he saw a letter written by the fugitive in 1890 and addressed to a friend of Tate's named Charles Green. It was mailed from Brazil.

Nothing more was heard from Tate and his ultimate fate remains a mystery. Considering that he was very much a family man who was unlikely to intentionally cease all contact with his loved ones,

79

Absconder

the most likely hypothesis is that in or around 1890, Tate was either murdered, committed suicide or died a natural death among strangers in a land far from home. In fact, in August 1890 the *New York Times* ran a story claiming that several of Tate's friends "who should know" believed he died in China.

Most of the judges and legislators who borrowed money from the treasury under Tate's reign repaid their loans very quickly once the light of public disclosure was upon them. Tate's bondsmen were freed from their debts by the state's appellate court in 1895. The case was labeled "Not to be officially reported," but word eventually got out to the public anyway. In *Kentucky: Decades of Discord,* historians Tapp and Klotter claim persuasively that the Tate scandal created an atmosphere of distrust in government that persists even now among the state's citizens.

Shakespeare wrote in *Julius Caesar* that the evil men do lives after them, and Tate serves as a fine illustration. His embezzlement of state funds affects Kentucky politics to this very day. First, the lawmakers created the office of state inspector and examiner to prevent such an occurrence from happening again. Then in 1890, two years after Honest Dick vanished, the legislature met to update the state's constitution. In 1891 legislators decided, because of Tate's performance, that elected officials cannot succeed themselves— that is, they can serve only one term. Kentucky remains one of the few states that still enforces this one-term limit.

Joseph Mulhattan

Hoaxer

This is the tale of Patrick Cunningham, a Madison County man who became famous unintentionally, but only for a few weeks, and for something he never actually did.

The story really must begin with a lengthy introduction to a fellow Kentucky citizen named Joseph Mulhattan, who should be recognized today as one of the great forgotten American humorists and pranksters of the late 19th century. Mulhattan was born in the vicinity of Pittsburgh, Pa., allegedly the son of a Presbyterian minister. (A biographical sketch written in 1888 claims Mulhattan was born around 1845, but the 1880 Jefferson County census places 1853 as the birth year.) After graduating from high school in Pittsburgh, he worked as a traveling salesman or "drummer" for a wholesale hardware firm of that city.

Around 1878, Mulhattan moved to Louisville, Ky., and worked for Hart and Company, a hardware, tool and cutlery manufacturer. He traveled for the company throughout the southern and southwestern United States. In 1886, another Louisville hardware firm, Rankins-Snyder, hired Mulhattan and sent him to Galveston, Texas. Mulhattan spent a year on the road in Texas and Mexico, but eventually he moved back to Kentucky and was hired in 1887 by a third Louisville hardware firm, Belknap and Company. He remained in the city for the next few years, except when on the road. The 1890 Louisville City Directory reveals that by then Mulhattan was general manager for Rankins-Snyder. For his entire stay in Louisville he boarded in Alexander's Hotel at the northwest corner of Seventh and Market Streets.

Like most itinerant peddlers, Mulhattan traveled on his beat through the southern states on his employer's behalf. However, unlike most of his brethren, he also had literary talent and a mischievous sense of humor, both of which combined with his love of alcohol to form memorable literature. His specialty was penning wild journalistic hoaxes with such convincing attention to detail, and delivered in such a deadpan fashion, that thousands of readers were often taken in. He had a true genius for making his flights of imagination seem believable, even when they contained absurdity piled on absurdity.

Mulhattan's *modus operandi* was to write his humbugs as they occurred to him while on his travels and then solemnly send them to newspapers, usually under the pseudonym Orange Blossom. He knew all too well that few newspapers would bother to make sure his sensational stories were accurate before rushing them into print. (Favorite targets were the *Pittsburgh Leader* and the *Philadelphia Public Ledger.)* Some papers seem to have knowingly printed his elaborate lies, recognizing them as circulation boosters.

Mulhattan became known as "the greatest liar in America." By 1888, his convincing fiction made him notorious enough to warrant inclusion in a collection of short biographies entitled *Prominent Men and Women of the Day* by Thomas W. Herringshaw. In that book, the "Champion Liar" kept company with such 19th-century luminaries as Mark Twain, Susan B. Anthony, Oscar Wilde, Czar Alexander III, Jules Verne, Sarah Bernhardt, William Gladstone, Sitting Bull, Frederick Douglass, Lord Tennyson and Walt Whitman, just to name a few. The author described Mulhattan's personality as clever, genial, tender-hearted and truthful except when joking. Physically, the great hoaxer was small (five-feet-five, 135 pounds), handsome, blue-eyed, a very fast talker and blessed with dark hair and beard. He was still a bachelor, "having, as he says, refused all offers of marriage and never made one."

Herringshaw related some of Mulhattan's literary adventures: "[His yarns are] are as entirely harmless as brilliant in conception and

Extremely rare portrait of Joe Mulhattan, hoaxer extraordinaire, circa 1888. From Herringshaw's *Biographical Review of Prominent Men and Women of the Day.*

treatment, such as only a pure-minded and educated gentleman of exceptional endowments can write. As a rule, they have been used without remuneration to the author, who has sometimes done graver work for the magazines and newspapers for pay, and with the conscientious regard for trustworthiness which characterizes all Mr. Mulhattan's merely business operations. Apart from these the genius takes wing and indulges in flights which amaze by the sublime range of their unveracity...."

Herringshaw added: "When the readers meet with a circumstantial account of hidden rivers being found here or there, of vast bodies of water deep under ground, the haunts of eyeless sharks and whales and other monsters who swim in its waters of untold depth, upon which icebergs float, he is exhorted to think of Mulhattan; and the ethnologist and geologist are warned against believing all they see in newspapers about newly discovered works by prehistoric man. How many persuasively written and circumstantial fabrics of lies Mr. Mulhattan has written probably only their author knows."

In late 1875, just before the nation's centennial, Mulhattan was able to convince countless readers that a campaign was under way to exhume the bodies of Washington and Lincoln, and have them placed on display so the public could pay 50 cents a head for the privilege of gawking at a couple of authentic American patriots. Mulhattan was particularly proud of this yarn; he referred to it as his "great national joke."

Another famous hoax was born when he wrote that Texas had been hit and set aflame by a meteor that was embedded 200 feet into the ground, and still left 70 feet of blistering hot stone to be seen above the surface. According to the writer, the disaster resulted in the deaths of people and cattle and destroyed innumerable houses and forests. "The *Fort Worth Gazette* published this incredible fabrication in collusion with its author," recounted Herringshaw. "An associated press agent read the account, in his hunger for news swallowed it, and telegraphed it to the main office in New York, from whence it was distributed the length of the United States. The morning after its universal publication, the *Gazette* received one hundred and fourteen telegrams of inquiry respecting the alleged phenomenon, of which several were from Europe; and letters asking for further information poured into the office for months."

On another occasion, Mulhattan wrote a fictitious account of the discovery of a carriage containing five skeletons on the Texas plains. "This little story had the distinction of being illustrated in several weekly publications, and is most devoutly believed by a great multitude which no man can number."

Some of the salesman's deceptions were quickly exposed, but others took on a life of their own. Though no solid proof has yet arisen, Mulhattan is thought by many to be the perpetrator of a famous fake news story about David Lang, purported to be a resident of Gallatin, Tn., who in 1880 disappeared into thin air while crossing a field, as "witnessed" by his wife, children, and a conveniently placed judge. Neither Lang nor the witnesses ever actually existed. The story is even now featured in collections of supposedly true paranormal occurrences. (The reader is invited to peruse *Stranger Than Science* by Frank Edwards, an unusually credulous journalist and broadcaster, for an account by a modern writer who fell for the Lang story. Also, see *Secrets Of The Supernatural*, by Kentuckian Joe Nickell, for an exposé.) The hardware salesman has also been credited with spreading the rumor that John Wilkes Booth escaped with his life and had been seen in various locations around the country. This, too, is a Mulhattan story that has had the durability of a galvanized steel casket.

(A couple of incidental biographical items: In 1884, a national convention of traveling salesmen meeting in Louisville, Mulhattan's city of residence, jokingly nominated him for president of the United States. The "Prince of Liars" pointed out in an interview that he expected to make a good showing since traveling salesmen could easily canvass the country and make stump speeches on his behalf from Maine to California. "We may carry a state or two, and thus throw the election into the House, and in that case the present political parties will have to compromise with us. I have always been a Democrat, but now I suppose I shall have to call myself the leader of the business men's reform party." Also, in 1883, Mulhattan helped organize the Kentucky Humane Society— no joke.)

Despite having been described as "a good man... highly esteemed wherever he is known," the great prankster appears to have had some genuine trouble with the law from time to time, having been arrested for stealing a roommate's money in Pittsburgh in 1891 and for public intoxication in Jeffersonville, In., in 1902. Upon his 1891 arrest, the *New York Times* dubbed him "Munchausen Mulhattan" and described his fame in this manner: "Joe Mulhattan is known in every city in the United States and has probably caused more trouble in newspaper offices than any other man in the country. His wild stories, written in the most plausible style, have more than once caused the special

correspondents of the progressive journals of the United States to hurry from coast to coast to investigate some wonderful occurrence which only existed in the imagination of the great liar."

But to return to Madison County's Patrick Cunningham. Somehow, possibly while traveling to or from his headquarters in Louisville, Mulhattan saw the following news account in the *Richmond Climax* of March 7, 1888:

"SNAKE BIT. Mr. Pat Cunningham, a plasterer of this place, went out to the home of Mr. R.P. McCord, in the Brookstown Community, last Tuesday. He accompanied two boys into the field to haul a load of fodder. When they had gotten a shock partially removed, a snake thrust its head up out of a hole in the ground that was under the shock, and bit Mr. Cunningham on the ankle, just above the shoe-top. He ran to the house, and Mrs. McCord gave him an antidote to rub on the wound. He limps a little yet, but will not die, although he was scared badly enough. This thing of a real snakebite in February is of rare occurrence. [Humorist] Josh Billings said: 'When I see a snaik in a hoal, I say to myself, 'that hoal belongs to that snaik.'"

Unpromising material for a literary hoax, one might think, but Mulhattan's imagination was fired by the item. Likely he noticed that Cunningham shared his first name with Saint Patrick, who drove the snakes out of Ireland. And, coincidentally, St. Patrick's Day was just a week away! Mulhattan rolled up his sleeves, got out pen and paper, and composed a ridiculous news story based *very* loosely on Cunningham's mishap. Then he sent it off, apparently anonymously, to the *Lexington Transcript* and awaited the result.

The fake story sported this opening paragraph: "The *Transcript* has received the following dispatch from Richmond, Ky.: Patrick Cunningham, of this place, is death to snakes and venomous reptiles of all kinds. The snake that bites him dies in great agony, frothing at the mouth, and swelling to almost double its former proportion. Cunningham has discovered a poison more deadly than that of the reptile, but harmless as a lotion for the human body, and the moment the fangs of the snake come in contact with it, a powerful electrical current is generated that drives the snake's own poison through every blood vessel in its body. Blood poisoning is the result, which, with the terrible electric shock causes almost instant death."

This set the tone for the entire piece. Perhaps feeling he was not being outrageous enough, Mulhattan further claimed Cunningham killed 17,000 rattlesnakes and black snakes in Madison County alone during the summer of 1887. Cunningham made several hundred dollars "by his wonderful skill in driving these offensive reptiles from the premises of our citizens." (The writer was careful to make it sound as if the article had been written by a Madison County resident.)

Mulhattan offered testimonial evidence. He wrote that J.B. Parks of Kingston hired Cunningham to rid his farm of snakes after the serpents killed several of his cows and chickens. Cunningham, who allegedly could "locate a den of snakes by their scent as easily as a dog can track a rabbit," smeared himself with his magical ointment and crawled into their den with a club. All those who bit him died horribly in the manner described above; the others were flattened by the laborer's club. Total body count on Parks' farm: 4,000 snakes.

Then there was the case of Richmond's Colonel Irvine, who went on a three-month vacation with his family. When he returned in September 1887, he found nearly empty two of the three barrels of Anderson County whisky he kept in his cellar. Well, empty may be putting it too strongly. One barrel contained 40 black snakes "in a beastly state of intoxication, while in the dark corners of the cellar groups of rattlesnakes were coiled, some sobering up, others in various states of intoxication." Mulhattan left it up to the reader's imagination just how one can determine whether a snake is drunk.

The colonel determined the vipers entered the cellar through a hole in the basement door, then crawled up the barrels and slipped one by one through the open bung holes. Left to their own devices, the snakes became hopeless alcoholics. We are solemnly assured in the article that Cunningham was summoned and made quick work of the slithering lushes, receiving $300 for killing 300 snakes. "Col. Shackelford, of the hardware firm of Shackelford and Gentry, owned half interest in the whisky destroyed by the snakes, and to that gentleman your reporter is indebted for these actual facts." (One wonders if perhaps the hoax was a collaboration between two members of the hardware-selling fraternity.)

But the anonymous Mulhattan was just getting warmed up. He included a long list of other notables who hired, or were about to hire, Cunningham to kill snakes for them: Col. Cobe Taylor, P.M. Pope, Claud Smith, Col. Prather, all of Madison County; J.W. Parris and Mayor Garner of Winchester; Col. De Long and Isaac Lumley of Lexington. Nearly all of the people mentioned in the article are listed in old census records. Mulhattan slyly included the names of actual citizens to add to the sense of verisimilitude.

The writer further noted that Madison County had been overrun with snakes in recent years. He offered the tongue-in-cheek hypothesis that the serpents had been so alarmed by the noise made at the Battle of Perryville in 1862 that they traveled *en masse* to quieter surroundings. Adding to the nonsense was his account of how Cunningham came by his snake-killing lotion: "He was born in India, near Calcutta. His parents were Irish and were sent out by the English Government for the department work in that province. It was in the jungles of India that Cunningham discovered from the natives the formula for making the deadly lotion so fatal to poisonous reptiles. The natives all anoint themselves with it and are thus rendered snake proof."

Mulhattan ended his article in typically audacious fashion: "Cunningham says he will keep on killing and driving the snakes until there is not one in the State of Kentucky, if the people will only pay him for it.... I have stated in this article nothing but actual facts, without the slightest attempt at exaggeration. If any of your readers doubt in the least they can address Col. Shackelford, of Shackelford & Gentry; F.W. Wiggins, of Wiggins & Breck; P.M. Pope, Esq.; Mr. Willis, the Postmaster, or any other reputable citizen of Richmond, or Mr. Cunningham himself, and they will find that the statements herein named are nothing but actual facts."

After receiving the bizarre article, the *Lexington Transcript* promptly ran it without doing any fact checking. The story was quickly picked up by wire services and appeared in papers across the United States. Some editors believed the tall tale wholeheartedly, while others perhaps suspected the hoax but went along with the joke in order to give their readers a good laugh.

In the end, several newspapers were embarrassed, their readers were either outraged or amused, and Joseph Mulhattan had another successful journalistic hoax to his credit. How Cunningham, Parks, Irvine, Shackelford and all the other people mentioned in the article felt about their sudden fame is unknown. It would be interesting to know whether they actually received any inquiring letters from gullible newspaper readers.

The story has a strange and delightful coda. The false news report spread as far away as Iowa, where it was read by the administrator of one John Cunningham, a relative of Patrick's. By coincidence, the administrator had been searching in vain for Patrick's current address. Several months previously, John Cunningham had died without wife or children and Patrick stood to inherit an estate of 3,000 acres of prime

Iowa land. In this unexpected manner, Mulhattan's hoax considerably enriched Patrick Cunningham's personal fortune.

Getting bitten by that snake may have been the luckiest thing that ever happened to him.

Henry Wooldridge

Monument Collector

It has been said, rather cynically, that the only way a man can sure-ly be immortal is to build a monument to himself. If this is true, Henry G. Wooldridge has earned immortality several times over. His burial site, located in Mayfield in Graves County, is one of the town's biggest tourist attractions. It is not difficult to locate within the cemetery, for Wooldridge's crowded plot is marked by no fewer than 16 different statues: two of himself, plus statues of several relatives and var-ious members of the animal kingdom, all placed there on Wooldridge's instructions before he died.

Wooldridge was born in Williamson County, Tn., on November 29, 1822, and moved to Mayfield in 1881, where he lived in the home of a niece. He gained a local reputation as a dyed-in-the-wool eccentric and infidel who scandalized his relatives by refusing to go to church. But Wooldridge was also wealthy, having made a fortune through horse breeding and trading. He also amassed sizable landhold-ings in the region. An avid hunter, he always had the finest horses and dogs money could purchase.

Though in excellent health in his later years, Wooldridge decid-ed to plan for the inevitable and bought a plot in Maplewood Cemetery. In 1892 he had a towering marble shaft-like tombstone erected, on which was carved his name, birthdate, a bas-relief picture of a horse and a Masonic emblem. He also had a vault built to contain his remains, complete with a carving of a rifle on the top.

These were expensive grave markers, but Wooldridge was not satisfied. One evening, family legend has it, he announced to his niece that he was going to have a statue of himself created and placed on his burial plot. As Mayfield chronicler Colonel Nathan Yates told the story, the niece protested that such a monument would be pretentious, and besides he had bigger things to be concerned with. "Uncle Henry, if I were you I'd think more about my soul before I died. Have you thought about your soul? Do you know where it's going when you die?" she asked.

Wooldridge was unfazed. "No. I don't know where my soul is going— I don't care— and I don't worry about it, but my body is going out to Maplewood Cemetery and I'm going to have a statue made of myself and when I die I'm going to be buried in a stone vault above ground— not in a grave."

"Uncle Henry, that's the silliest thing I ever heard of. You've got no business building a statue to yourself— you're not famous," responded the niece.

Wooldridge replied with impeccable logic. "I'm not famous, but I've got the money to build the statue." And with that, he began making arrangements with a monument works in nearby Paducah. Wooldridge insisted the statue be made of marble, so the firm sent a photo of the obsessed man to a commissioned Italian sculptor, who obtained the marble and did the actual carving at a cost of $1,000.

When the statue arrived from Italy early in 1893, it was taken to Maplewood Cemetery and placed atop Wooldridge's grave. The statue features its subject standing beside a pedestal with his hand atop a book that many thought "looked suspiciously like a Bible," as related by Yates. It was judged by all to be an excellent likeness, and Wooldridge was very proud of his new monument beside the shaft and vault.

But he was still unsatisfied. As grand as the marble statue was, it really said nothing about the man himself. Perhaps another statue would properly reveal the Wooldridge personality! He was always an animal lover, especially of horses. Why not a statue of himself riding Fop, his favorite horse? He decided it must be done immediately, and

again contacted the stone carvers in Paducah.

This time the monument firm informed Wooldridge that his next statue could be made right there in Paducah, using sandstone in place of marble. Wooldridge agreed, and the company hired a renowned local sculptor named William Lydon to do the work, again using only a photo of Wooldridge. He requested that the horse be 15 hands high.

It took Lydon nine weeks to carve the figures out of an 11-ton block of stone imported from southern Indiana. The finished work weighed two and a half tons and had to be sent to Mayfield via a special railroad flatcar with air brakes. After the carving of Wooldridge and Fop was set up behind the Italian statue in May 1893, Wooldridge rode out to Maplewood Cemetery to view Lydon's handiwork. Reportedly he said, "That's me, that's me," and headed back to town without even getting out of the carriage for a closer look.

Perhaps Wooldridge's relatives thought by now his thirst for grave markers was surely quenched. If so, they were wrong. Although Wooldridge was delighted with his stone likenesses, something troubled him. As a lifelong bachelor, he had no children to carry on the family name. His brothers and sisters were all dead, and he wanted the other members of the Wooldridge family to be remembered. They should have statues on his plot as well.

From this point, new statues began appearing on Wooldridge's burial site the way toadstools spring up on the graves of others. He commissioned the Paducah plant to carve statues of his parents, to be placed beside his marble image; they provided two generic statues, since Wooldridge had no photos to give them for reference. Wooldridge did not mind this at all, and asked for stone images of his three brothers, John, William and Alfred. Sculptor Lydon obliged with three identical statues of men with their arms held stiffly at their sides. These were placed near the front of the procession.

At the back end of this mob of statues are three sandstone sculptures of women. These were created in Mayfield by a local carver of tombstones. Unlike the three brothers, the three women feature variations in hand positions and clothing, but the faces are identical. Exactly whom the three statues represent varies from story to story. Some claim they are Wooldridge's three sisters; others are certain the statues are of two sisters and a woman named Susan Neely. (Romantic legend has it that Neely, of Franklin, Tn., was Wooldridge's only true love. They were engaged to be married when he was young, but she died of injuries incurred in a horseback riding accident. Allegedly, the avowed bachelor wore her engagement ring to the end of his days.)

In addition, there are two more human figures, both little girls. One statue is of a great-niece, Minnie, who once attended the old man when he was ill. The other is of Maude Reed, the daughter of a woman in whose home Wooldridge once boarded. She is depicted peering at a scroll and stands near the rear of Fop the horse. To commemorate his love for hunting, Wooldridge added four more statues: his favorite foxhound, Bob, a deerhound named Tow Head, and of course a fox and a deer for them to chase through all eternity.

Wooldridge's generally excellent health took a turn for the worse around 1898, when he suffered a stroke that left half of his body paralyzed. Nevertheless, he continued planning to have more statues added to the strange entourage. His mania was ended only by his death on

May 30, 1899. The final count: one vault, one marble shaft and 16 statues at a cost of around $6,000, all squeezed into an area that measures 17 by 33 feet.

Despite the cramped conditions in the plot, Wooldridge's body is the only one that lies there. Before his death he bought a burial robe and a made-to-order walnut casket. However, when his casket was being pushed into the vault, it was found to be about seven inches too long to fit. Relatives decided to have the vault enlarged. Wooldridge would have been pleased.

Today the Wooldridge monuments rank among Mayfield's best-known curiosities and are listed on the National Register of Historic Places. A chain link fence was built around the plot to thwart vandals and other cretins after a tail was snapped off of one of the dog statues and the antlers disappeared from the deer's head. The monuments will remain for centuries as a reminder of the vision of one man who, believing his own soul was not immortal, wanted to find a way to keep loved ones near him always.

William Goebel

Assassinated Governor

Some governors are remembered for their daring reforms; others are remembered for their spectacular incompetence. But Kentucky's Governor Goebel is remembered today primarily for being the only state governor in American history to have been assassinated while in office. Goebel's murder remains unsolved, and because there is considerable evidence a conspiracy was afoot among his political enemies, in some ways Goebel might be considered Kentucky's own version of John F. Kennedy.

Goebel, son of German immigrants, was born in Sullivan County, Pa., on January 4, 1856, but grew up in Covington, Ky. His life could have served as a model American success story: faced with wretched poverty in his childhood, Goebel worked his way into law school, and after making a sizable fortune as a lawyer he gradually turned to politics. In 1887, he became a member of the Kentucky State Senate when he was only 31. Neither especially well-liked nor a powerful orator, it was widely suspected that he rose to the top by indulging in machine-style politics. His image was tarnished when in 1895 he got into a public fight with a banker named John Sanford in Covington after publishing an article with a scurrilous reference to Sanford in a local newspaper. (The ever charming Goebel had referred to Sanford as "Gonorrhea John.") The men exchanged gunfire almost simultaneous-

Statue of Governor William Goebel in front of the Old Capitol Building, Frankfort, Ky. *Photo by Kyle McQueen.*

ly, but while Goebel escaped injury, Sanford received a fatal shot to the head. The murder was judged to have been committed in self defense, and Goebel served no time for it.

Goebel continued rising in politics not because of his personality, but in spite of it. Variously described as coldly intellectual, aloof, overly ambitious, power-hungry, ruthless and arrogant, he had a knack for making political enemies, especially through his constant attacks on

97

Assassinated Governor

the powerful railroad industry; the Louisville and Nashville line in particular was a subject of Goebel's wrath. Nevertheless, the reform-minded Goebel had a certain appeal to the "common voter"— some enemies uncharitably called him a demagogue— and by 1899, he had become so prominent in state politics that he received the Democratic party's nomination for governor. He did indeed subsequently become Kentucky's governor, but only after an extremely controversial and contentious election process. Following a bitter campaign that had been characterized by personal insults and threats of violence from both political parties, when the votes were counted Goebel had lost by a scant 2,383 votes. His Republican opponent, William Sylvester Taylor, was sworn in as governor in December.

Having lost the race by such a narrow margin the Democrats, who had a majority of votes in the legislature, demanded the votes be scrutinized, hinting that the election had been fixed and charging that voters in Louisville had been coerced into casting their ballots for Taylor. Goebel also claimed that illegal ballots had been used in 40 counties, and that the L & N railroad forced its employees to vote for Taylor. Governor Taylor and the Republicans were infuriated by the suggestion, and regarded Goebel as a poor loser who was trying to change the outcome of a fair election and thwart the will of the voters.

Journalist Urey Woodson, a personal friend of Goebel's, remembered that on January 29, 1900, he was sitting with the politician in his room at the Capitol Hotel. Woodson asked Goebel what he would do if the legislature determined he rightfully should be declared governor. Goebel responded that he would have a grand jury indict Milton Smith, president of the L & N railroad, Basil Duke, the railroad's lobbyist, and *Louisville Post* editor Dick Knott on a charge of criminal libel, and send them to jail if he could. Suddenly there was a knock on the door, which Goebel answered. An unidentified man stepped in and confidentially related that on his train ride to Frankfort he had overheard a number of mountaineers discussing a plot to assassinate Goebel. After the man hurried from the room, Goebel remarked, "I must go to the Senate every morning and attend to my official duties. I shall not hide or shirk. I have been hearing these stories that somebody was going to kill me ever since last summer and I have gotten to the point where, if I can

Offbeat Kentuckians

only live to be sworn in as governor, I don't care a damn what then happens."

The very next day, January 30, 1900, despite the palpable threat of violence that was in the air, Goebel chose to walk rather than ride to the Capitol building in Frankfort accompanied only by two cronies, Jack Chinn and Eph Lillard, rather than a squad of bodyguards. He was on his way to a special legislative body that had convened to investigate the gubernatorial election. However, at 11:15 a.m., just as the group reached the halfway point between the outdoor water fountain and the steps of the Capitol, the sound of gunfire echoed through the cold winter air. The person firing the weapon used smokeless powder to avoid being easily spotted by onlookers. Goebel, who was about 50 feet from the Executive Building, was struck in the chest. A bullet of small caliber, not over .38, pierced his lung and he fell mortally wounded to the sidewalk. The fatal bullet, after exiting Goebel's back, lodged in a hackberry tree some distance behind the fallen governor.

As with the assassination of JFK many years later, in the aftermath there would be much contradiction concerning the number of rifle shots and the exact location from which they were fired. Contemporary newspaper accounts related that five shots were fired, but several months later while testifying in court, Chinn claimed to have heard six. It was agreed the bullets were fired from the State

Building, located 50 feet east of the Capitol, but while Lillard thought the shots came from the first floor, some papers claimed it was the second floor, and other accounts have the shots coming from both the second and third floors. If a well-organized conspiracy to kill Goebel existed, conceivably there could have been assassins on all three floors. Journalist Woodson theorized that only the first shot was intended to hit Goebel, and the others were "fired to mislead and mystify" witnesses.

Conspiracy-minded individuals later claimed that at least one bullet came from Secretary of State Caleb Powers' office on the first floor, although a reliable *New York Times* article dated January 31 asserted that at the time of the shots, Powers's office was occupied by men "who rushed to the window as soon as the shots were heard, and all of them declare that there was no shot fired from that part of the building." For what it may be worth, the same article asserted that the shots were definitely fired from the window in the center of the third story, noting that upon investigation the window was still raised about eight inches, "no effort having been made to close it by the would-be assassin."

At any rate, only one bullet hit Goebel but it was sufficient. Reportedly, Chinn asked, "Are you hurt, Goebel?" The wounded man replied, "They have got me this time. I guess they have killed me." Chinn, Lillard and some bystanders carried Goebel to the office of Dr. E.E. Hume in the basement of the Capitol Hotel. Kentucky's state historian James Klotter succinctly described the chaos that reigned in Frankfort for the next few days as the wounded Goebel was being treated: "Governor Taylor declared a state of insurrection, called out the militia, and ordered the legislature to reconvene in London, a Republican area." The Democrats thought this unconstitutional and refused to do so.

While Goebel was on his deathbed on the second floor of the Capitol Hotel, the special legislative session (which consisted almost entirely of Democrats) met in secret and determined that he had been correct all along and rightfully should have been declared governor. He was sworn in on January 31. In turn, Republicans protested that this was illegal. The result was that, as Klotter states, "Another militia appeared, and two governments, each with its own army, existed" in the streets of Frankfort. Though now largely forgotten, this was certainly one of the greatest internal political crises in the history of Kentucky, if not the nation. For a time it even seemed as though a civil war might be possible.

Goebel's victory was pyrrhic, to say the least. Despite the attentions of 18 physicians, he died of his wounds at 6:44 p.m. on February 3, leaving behind neither widow nor children. His final words, according to the Democrats, were "Tell my friends to be brave, fearless and loyal to the great common people." (More skeptical persons, such as the Kentucky journalist and humorist Irvin S. Cobb, claimed that his final words actually concerned his last meal: "Doc, that was a damned bad oyster.")

Goebel's only official act while governor had been to call off the militia. He was succeeded in office by his lieutenant governor, John Crepps Wickliffe Beckham, but still the Republicans would not concede that Goebel should ever have been governor. (The question was eventually settled by the U. S. Supreme Court, which ruled in Goebel's favor on May 21, 1900.)

The unanswered question is: who shot William Goebel? Conspiracy theories were advanced immediately after the assassination and several suspects have emerged over the years. Some observers whispered that the powerful railroad industry, which truly hated Goebel, had seen to the elimination of its biggest enemy. During the election, the L & N railroad had spent a half-million dollars trying to defeat Goebel. When their efforts failed, could they have decided on more drastic measures?

The first man arrested for the murder was Harland Whittaker (some sources give his first name as Holland), a farmer from Butler County, which was Governor Taylor's home county. Whittaker was heavily armed with three revolvers and a knife and was found in the vicinity of the shooting, but he protested that he was running toward the scene of the crime when apprehended. An examination of his weaponry revealed no used cartridges and no traces of powder residue. Furthermore, witnesses declared the shots they heard came from a rifle, not a revolver. Despite there being no real evidence against him,

Whittaker was arrested and sent to a jail in Louisville. He was held without bail for several weeks and even taken to trial, until it became clear to everyone that he was guilty of nothing more than being an armed Republican in the wrong place at the wrong time.

The most prominent suspect in the assassination was former Governor Taylor. Shortly after Goebel's death, Taylor was widely suspected of being behind the conspiracy, and was even indicted for it, but he swiftly moved to Indiana before charges could be filed. The governor of that state refused to extradite Taylor, so he was never forced to divulge publicly what he knew, if anything, of the plot to kill Goebel. He was officially pardoned by Kentucky's Republican Governor Augustus Willson in April 1909.

Although Taylor's flight seems suspicious at first glance, his supporters believed the charges against him were unfounded and were simply a political grandstanding ploy from the Democrats. Possibly he fled the state not to avoid arrest, but because of the threats which certainly were being made against him. In support of this theory, it is known that for some time immediately after Goebel's death, Taylor surrounded himself with armed bodyguards for fear of being assassinated and was afraid even to leave his own office. In addition, Taylor had his wife and children guarded by 30 soldiers. His fear of being killed was so great that he even considered resigning. After Taylor fled to Indiana, he became a prominent lawyer in Indianapolis. But it seems inconceivable that officials in Indiana would have refused to extradite Taylor if there had been any solid evidence linking him to a high profile murder.

Although Taylor was out of reach, other suspects were swiftly collared. Several indictments were made among state employees. Most were tried by Judge James Cantrill, a pro-Goebel Democrat who made rulings flagrantly prejudiced against the Republicans on trial. In addition, the juries were invariably made up of suspiciously high numbers of Democrats; out of a jury pool of 368 men, only eight were Republicans. This led many to believe that the Democrats considered the trials payback time against Republicans to avenge both the death of Goebel and the stealing of the election. In the end, out of 16 indictments, only three men were convicted by the grand jury for conspiring to kill William Goebel. The first was Caleb Powers of Knox County,

Republican secretary of state. The second was James B. Howard of Clay County, who had recently been indicted for murdering one George "Baldy" Baker in the notorious White-Baker family feud in his home county. Howard happened to be in Frankfort on the day of the assassination to seek a pardon from Governor Taylor. The Democrats claimed Howard was the actual trigger man, and that Powers had offered him the pardon in exchange for killing Goebel. The third accused man was Henry Youtsey of Newport, a clerk in the office of the state auditor, described by author John Ed Pearce as "excitable [and] obviously unbalanced."

All three were convicted by the pro-Goebel Democratic juries on flimsy evidence, including testimony from unreliable witnesses. Indeed, during Powers' trial, one witness admitted under oath that attorney Thomas Campbell and Goebel's brother Arthur had threatened him with life imprisonment if he did not testify against Powers. Nevertheless, Powers was sentenced to life in prison; Howard, who Democrats believed undertook the assassination for a payment of $1600, was given the death penalty; and Youtsey was given life in prison. The attorneys for Powers and Howard appealed their verdicts. Youtsey, who did not appeal, was sent to prison to begin serving his sentence.

A later change in the political climate benefited Powers and Howard. By the time their cases were heard on appeal, the two accused conspirators faced an appellate court consisting largely of Republican judges, who consistently overturned their convictions and ordered new trials. However, they still faced juries that were overwhelmingly Democratic, so Powers was tried three more times, and Howard twice more.

After several legal twists and turns, the two supposed conspirators at last received some lucky breaks. Judge Cantrill was forced to disqualify himself from presiding over their trials owing to his obvious bias against the defendants. Also, a Republican governor, Augustus Willson, had been elected in 1907. He pardoned the two men in 1908.

The third of the supposed conspirators, the stenographer Youtsey, was widely believed by many to be the actual assassin. It came out during his trial that he had purchased specially-made bullets before the shooting. The prosecution claimed that Youtsey and his co-conspirators thought Goebel wore a bulletproof vest. Ex-governor Taylor's secretary claimed during Powers's first trial that he had seen Youtsey engaging in suspicious behavior— specifically, looking out an office window while holding a rifle, and making the cryptic remark "If trouble comes, I am going to be prepared." In addition, a witness came forth during Powers' final trial, testifying that he owned a Marlin rifle that was the murder weapon. He claimed the former owner of the gun had purchased it directly from Youtsey. However, none of the evidence against Youtsey was strong enough to keep him in prison, and after serving several years of his life sentence, he was paroled by Governor James Black, a Democrat, in 1916. He was officially pardoned in 1919. Because of

The coat Goebel wore when he was shot. Note bullet hole in the back.
Courtesy Kentucky Historical Society Museum.

all the contradictory court testimony, it will probably be forever unknown whether Powers, Howard and Youtsey actually had inside knowledge about the assassination. Both Howard and Youtsey were still vehemently denying the accusations as late as 1939.

Perhaps the unlikeliest of all the suspects in the shooting was none other than Jack Chinn, one of the two men who had been walking to the Capitol with Goebel when he was shot. Showing a fine disregard for all the eyewitness testimony and ballistics evidence, Mrs. Kate Banta of Frankfort started telling people that she personally saw Chinn shoot Goebel in the back. Chinn was not amused by Banta's absurd hypothesis and filed a libel suit in March 1900, demanding $25,000 in damages.

Several years after Goebel's death, a brand new suspect turned up when a Mrs. Lulu Clark announced in September 1907 that she knew who the real killer was. Clark, whose maiden name was Lulu Williams, was from Rothwell, Menifee County, Ky., but had lived for years at Mt. Sterling. She told the following remarkable tale.

On the day of the shooting, she and a female cousin named Gertrude King were approaching the rear entrance to the State House in Frankfort. A man was standing in the doorway whom they recognized as John Sanford of Covington— son of the man Goebel had killed years before in a gunfight. Clark claimed that her cousin Gertrude and John Sanford were dating at the time. The women were startled by the sudden sound of gunfire, and shortly thereafter a man who looked "like a mountaineer" and brandished a rifle ran out of the building. In the presence of the two women, the man said to Sanford, "I got the — — — —," as the newspapers delicately phrased it. Clark recognized the "mountaineer" as a friend of hers named Turner Igo, a merchant who lived in Farmers, Rowan County. Igo and Sanford ran to a fence, where the latter inexplicably gave the assassin a pair of boots he had been carrying. After Igo put on the new pair, the two men fled the scene.

In addition, Mrs. Clark claimed that on January 25, five days before the shooting, she had seen Igo at a train depot in Mt. Sterling, where he freely admitted to her that he intended to kill Goebel, and when she met him again in Jeffersonville, In., after the assassination, "he reminded her that he had fulfilled his promise." As if to add more smoke to the smoking gun, Clark furthermore stated that Sanford had also confessed to her cousin Gertrude a few days before the murder that Goebel was as good as dead. He said, "Here is my chance to get revenge. The legislature has met."

Clark swore to all of this in an affidavit which was taken on April 11, 1907, in the Indianapolis law office of Kentucky's ex-Governor William Taylor. If true, then the man behind the assassination of Goebel was none other than the son of the man Goebel himself had killed, and the apparent motive was personal vengeance rather than politics. But *was* the story true?

Alas, Clark's claims began to unravel almost immediately. It was pointed out that Igo had been deceased three or four years, and thus was not able to defend himself against her charges. The dead man's cousin Samuel Igo stepped forward to note that he had never heard of Lulu Williams Clark, and further, "I never heard of [Turner Igo's] acquaintance with Sanford nor any hint that my cousin was ever connected even remotely with Goebel's death." Gertrude King was also dead, and therefore could not corroborate Clark's version of events. Commonwealth's Attorney R. B. Franklin revealed that, among other things, none of the witnesses for the defense or the prosecution reported seeing two women at the State House back steps, and that the door which Clark asserted she and her cousin were heading toward actually led to a men's toilet in the basement. There weren't even any outside steps leading to that particular door.

Then Sanford himself denounced the story, stating categorically that he had never known Clark, King, or Igo. He was able to prove that at the time of the assassination he had been living with a number of army officers while on business in the Philippines. Lulu Clark had even gotten his name wrong; it was Cassius Marshall Sanford, not John. Another promising lead in solving the Goebel mystery died ignominiously.

Perhaps, as with JFK's assassination, some of the conspiracy theories are too elaborate for their own good. The true killers of Goebel may have been nothing more than anonymous thugs acting on their own volition. Klotter has noted that while the hotly contested election

Offbeat Kentuckians

was being debated in the legislature, Frankfort was occupied by "numerous armed men, mostly Republicans from eastern Kentucky." Perhaps one of them simply saw his chance and took it, then slipped out of town and into obscurity.

The mystery remains, as do traces of the man himself. In front of the old Capitol building in Frankfort, a statue of the ill-fated governor looks blandly at passersby, his stone arms folded in a defiant stance across his chest. His pompous alleged final words are engraved on the base. The Kentucky Historical Society's new museum displays Goebel's coat, the hole left by the fatal bullet clearly visible. On the 100th anniversary of the assassination, the Scott County Museum in Georgetown had a special exhibit featuring Goebel political memorabilia, bullets, photos, furniture used in the courtroom during the trials of the three accused conspirators and even a .38-caliber pearl-handled revolver Goebel was carrying when he was shot. We can stare at the reminders, but a century later, we are no closer to having a solution to the crime than Kentuckians were in 1900.

Plaque on sidewalk in front of the Old Capitol Building, Frankfort.
Photo by author.

Carry Nation

Militant Prohibitionist

It is June 7, 1900, in Kiowa, Kansas. You are sitting peacefully in Dobson's Saloon, sipping a cold beer on a hot day, thinking perhaps about the models in the latest Sears catalog. Suddenly the establishment's swinging doors burst open. Into the room steps an enormous woman— six feet tall, weighing 175 pounds— clad almost completely in black. Her silver hair is pulled back; she looks like she could be anyone's grandmother. But this matronly woman is not smiling. Behind the steel-rimmed spectacles her eyes flash with self-righteous anger. For the first time you notice she is carrying a bag full of rocks. Glaring, she addresses the patrons: "Men, I have come to save you from a drunkard's fate!"

With that, she begins tossing the rocks at customers' glasses with the accuracy of a professional baseball pitcher while singing hymns. Patrons are ducking under the tables, desperately trying to avoid flying shards of glass. A mirror becomes a casualty. Then the woman aims her stones at the bottles of liquor on the shelves. She does not stop until every bottle is smashed and the valuable liquids are draining through the cracks in the floor. When her work is done, the woman turns to the proprietor and says matter-of-factly, "Now, Mr. Dobson, I have finished. God be with you." She storms out of the building, leaving behind piles of broken glass, cowering customers and

Carry Nation.
Courtesy Library of Congress,
LC-USZ62-60404.

a bartender incredulously shaking his head.

You have just met Carry Nation, a prohibitionist who is not content merely to talk about the evils of drink. And you have had the dubious honor of being present at her very first saloon smashing.

Nation's busy morning was hardly over. After making quick work of Dobson's Saloon, Carry climbed into her buggy, which was loaded down with rocks she collected at her homestead at Medicine Lodge, 20 miles away. She drove to the other two saloons in Kiowa and did to them what she did at Dobson's. When the sheriff approached her, undoubtedly thinking she had gone insane, Nation asked— no, demanded— that he arrest her. Instead, the town officials asked her to please leave town, probably realizing that she had simply destroyed something that legally should not have been there anyway.

It wasn't long before the name Carry Nation was on the nation's lips. Some called her a fanatical busybody with no regard for the personal property of others, a vigilante for temperance. Some called her an avenging angel who boldly took action against demon alcohol with no thought of her own safety. She called herself "a bulldog running along at the feet of Jesus, barking at what He doesn't like."

Nation was a Kentucky girl, having been born Carry Amelia Moore near Lancaster in Garrard County on November 25, 1846. Her father, George Moore, was a teetotaling planter who was emotionally distant from his children. Insanity ran rampant in her mother's side of the family; Nation's maternal grandmother, an uncle, an aunt and several cousins were all mentally ill. Nation's mother, Mary Campbell Moore, did not escape the burden dictated by genetics. She suffered from bouts of mental illness, sometimes believing she was Queen Victoria. (Much later, Nation's only daughter was also destined to go insane.) As a child, Nation herself was often chronically depressed.

Adding to the child's instability, the Moores moved frequently. In 1851, when Nation was five years old, the family moved first to Boyle County, then to Woodford County. From there, the Moores traveled west to Grayson County, Tx., and finally settled in Belton, Mo. around 1865. Nation's mother spent the last years of her life in the Missouri State Hospital for the Insane, dying there on September 24, 1893.

Not long after moving to Belton, the Moores took in a boarder, Dr. Charles Gloyd. Young Nation fell in love with the doctor, and they wed on November 21, 1867, much against her father's will.

The Gloyds moved to the town of Holden, and the young bride soon realized what a mistake she had made when she married the doctor. Gloyd was an alcoholic who preferred drinking with his friends at the Masonic lodge to spending time with his wife. This spawned two of Nation's lifelong obsessive hatreds: alcohol and the Masons. After only a few months, she moved back into her parents' home with her newborn daughter, Charlien. The doctor drank himself to death less than six months afterwards. Nation later wrote, "The world was like a place of torture. I know now that the impulse was born in me then to combat to the death this inhumanity to man."

The widow became a schoolteacher, but lost her job in 1877 to the niece of a school board member. Shortly thereafter she married David Nation, nearly twenty years her senior, a lawyer, minister and editor of the *Warrensburg Journal.* This marriage was destined to last much longer than the one to Gloyd, but would be little happier. The couple moved to Richmond, Tx., around 1881, where Carry Nation tried to run a hotel. Business was slow because her religious beliefs induced her to forbid drinking and smoking on the premises. In 1889, the Nations moved to Medicine Lodge, Ks.

Though Kansas was officially a dry state, saloons studded the landscape. Nation found this intolerable and formed a local chapter of the Women's Christian Temperance Union and made it her personal mission to drive the saloons out of Kansas. She felt she was chosen by God to perform this important task. After all, Jesus Christ once came to her in a vision and told her that at the wedding feast of Cana described in the Gospels, He had actually changed the water into grape juice, not intoxicating wine. She even saw religious symbolism in her very name, convinced as she was that Carry A. Nation would carry a nation to temperance.

At first the women of the WCTU were content merely to protest the sale of alcohol. But as time passed, their leader became more outspoken. She took to greeting saloonkeepers with such conversation-killing salutations as "Good morning, destroyer of men's souls," or "How do you do, maker of drunkards and widows?" She procured an ancient hand organ and would loudly serenade the proprietors of saloons and their customers with hymns.

And then her behavior became *strange.* One day after a prayer session, Nation later claimed, she heard a voice from an invisible source whisper "Take something in your hands and throw it at those places and smash them." She obeyed the voice and demolished Dobson's Saloon and two others with stones, as previously described. A few hours after she triumphed over Kiowa's saloons, a tornado swept through eastern Kansas, doing much property damage. Nation took this as a good omen, and on December 27, 1900, she rode to the Hotel Carey in Wichita bent on righteous destruction.

She entered the building with a long iron rod, an armload of rocks and a prodigious amount of energy. In just a few minutes, Nation destroyed not only bottles of liquor, but also mirrors, windows, the bar, wood paneling and a painting she deemed pornographic entitled "Cleopatra At The Bath," loudly preaching the Gospel all the while. Even this did not quell her zeal, and she jerked cigarettes out of the mouths of men staring agog and stomped them (the cigarettes, that is) into the floor.

This time Nation got her fondest wish. She was arrested. She stayed in the Wichita jail a little over two weeks, receiving hundreds of pieces of fan mail and hate letters. The publicity made her instantly famous coast to coast. Biographer Herbert Asbury noted her influence: "Even Carry Nation's enemies were compelled to acknowledge that her extraordinary methods had produced definite and concrete results, for in less than six months she had done more to enforce the prohibition laws than had been accomplished in 20 years by the ineffectual campaigns of the churches and temperance organizations."

When Nation went home after humiliating Wichita's barkeeps and town officials, her husband facetiously recommended that she use a hatchet next time for doing maximum damage. Nation reportedly replied, "That's the most sensible thing you have said since I married you."

On January 21, 1901, she returned to Wichita with the weapon that would make her the most famous American woman to wield a hatchet since Lizzie Borden. (In later years, Nation owned a trio of hatchets named Faith, Hope and Charity.) With three other women from the local WCTU named Wilhoit, Muntz and Evans, Nation headed for James Burnes' saloon. Her fame preceded her. When the patrons saw her coming, they fled the building. The four women began smashing and chopping with almost military precision, and when Evans was badly wounded by flying glass, the women were only inspired to smash even harder. Fifteen minutes later, when the building's contents were demolished, Nation proclaimed without a trace of irony "Peace on earth, good will to men." Then they left for the barroom at John Herrig's Palace Cafe, where they commenced smashing and left only after Herrig threatened to blow out Nation's brains with a revolver. Following this abortive attempt, the women set off to re-destroy what remained of the Hotel Carey's saloon. By the time they arrived, a crowd of 3,000 had gathered to cheer or boo her every move. But no further destruction occurred that day. After a struggle with the police, during which Nation tried to hit a detective with a poker, the four women were hauled away in a wagon while singing "Nearer, My God, To Thee."

Ignoring the fact that she was already in trouble with the law, Nation packed her weapon and made plans to perform "hatchetation," as she liked to call it, in the towns of Enterprise and Topeka. But as she was about to leave Wichita, Sheriff Simmons informed her that she was under arrest. She responded to this news by slapping him and wringing his ears before a crowd. By the time backup arrived, Nation was dragging the sheriff by the ears all around the train station's waiting room. She was thrown into the county jail, but released on bond the next day.

It should be noted that many temperance advocates disapproved of Nation and her violent escapades. For example, when Nation first started gaining notoriety in January 1901, the president of the Kansas WCTU, Mrs. A.M. Hutchinson, assured the press that "Loyalty to Mrs. Nation demands that we procure for her a fair trial, but we do not favor her methods." When she visited San Antonio in October 1904, the local Reform League offered to pay her if she would leave town and stop raiding saloons. Perhaps the fact that she had yanked the mayor's cigar out of his mouth and stuck the lit end in his ear had something to do with it.

However, to many other women she was an inspiration, and soon other temperance advocates across America were also visiting their local saloons armed with Bible and hatchet. (One of her followers, Myra McHenry, would get into serious trouble in Hutchinson, Ks., in 1905 for throwing rocks at hecklers.)

Nation was not content to rest on her laurels. Traveling outside of Kansas, she continued smashing saloons, getting arrested, lecturing crowds and assembled lawmakers and fighting for public morality in ways some considered mentally unbalanced. When President McKinley was assassinated, she hinted strongly that she had no sympathy for him because he was a friend of the brewers and was a smoker besides. She called President Theodore Roosevelt "blood-thirsty, reckless, and a cigarette-smoking rummy," and took a trip to the White House to browbeat him into giving up tobacco and Masonry. (She was denied access.) Stylishly dressed women were "mannikins hung with the filthy rags of fashion."

When she visited Washington, she burst unannounced into the United States Senate chamber, shook her hatchet at the alarmed lawmakers and screamed "Anarchy! Conspiracy! Treason! Discuss those!" In Crawfordsville, In., she gave shiny new hatchets to a group of children and watched with pride as the rosy-cheeked marauders entered and smashed a saloon. She built a sort of halfway house in Kansas City for "rum widows" called the Home for Drunkards' Wives and Mothers. In November 1902, Nation made a scene at a horse show in Madison Square Garden when she loudly and pointedly told the fiancee of a Vanderbilt that her dress was immodest. Toward the end of her career she fought a losing battle to sober up the rowdy students at Harvard and Yale.

She even had the nerve to terrorize the heavyweight boxer John L. Sullivan in the New York saloon where he was proprietor. He had previously boasted that if she came to his establishment he would drop her down the sewer. When she showed up to call his bluff, Sullivan made himself scarce.

If not even John L. Sullivan could face Carry Nation, what chance did her husband have? Her antics took a toll on the marriage, and in November 1901 David Nation divorced her on grounds of cruelty and desertion. He complained to the newspapers that she was dom-

ineering, embarrassed him publicly and had conversations at night with an invisible Jesus Christ.

Not everyone took Nation's bad-attitude sobriety meekly, and in fact some of her intended targets fought back. She was beaten and horsewhipped by a female bartender in Enterprise, Ks., in January 1901, after which angry citizens pelted Nation with rotten eggs and chased her out of town. A couple of days later in Topeka, the wife of a saloonkeeper thrashed Nation about the head with a broomstick, and then a mob gave her a sound beating even though she was surrounded by four bodyguards. In April 1902, a Nebraska City barkeep punched her twice in the face and threw her out in the street. The *San Francisco Examiner* of October 13, 1904, reports that gamblers in San Antonio were so infuriated when she commenced breaking their roulette wheels that they shot at her feet, and "she was forced to dance the first jig of her life." After she left the gambling den she went to a saloon to indulge in smashing, but the bartender threw a bungstarter at her stomach. In July 1904, an Elizabethtown, Ky., bartender named J. R. Neighbors brained her with a chair. Reportedly, a police officer watched the event with considerable interest, but neither interfered nor arrested the attacker. A saloon owner named Charles Aiello of Trinidad, Col., was so rough when he threw Nation out of his bar one fine day in October 1906 that she swallowed her false teeth. They became lodged in her throat and she nearly choked to death.

Alcohol, incidentally, was not the only vice that obsessed Nation. She also preached against tobacco, pornography, scandalous fashions and the evils of the corset. But it was her fight against demon rum that made her a living legend. On the other hand, it is often forgotten that she also crusaded in favor of the homeless and equal rights for women.

Gradually Nation parlayed her notoriety into a small cottage industry, with most of the proceeds going to pay her bail and many fines. She sold tiny souvenir hatchets made of pewter, a bi-weekly paper called *The Smasher's Mail,* a nearly incoherent autobiography written in 1904, and a newspaper entitled *The Hatchet.* At one point she and her favorite weapon even starred in a vaudeville act, a rewritten version of that hoary temperance play "Ten Nights In A Barroom." The climactic scene featured Nation wreaking havoc with dozens of prop bottles on a saloon set. Nation insisted the title of the play be changed to "Hatchetation."

Nation's hold on the public imagination eventually faltered. When she first began her forays against liquor, her defiant methods won many supporters. But after a few years of constant violence, arrests, and harangues, the balance of opinion shifted against her. She was seen more as a nuisance and a lunatic than a conquering hero. Soon her only noticeable supporters were other fanatics.

In 1908 Nation decided the British Isles were in need of her special brand of activism, so she set sail on the steamship *Columbia*. During the voyage across the Atlantic, she kept her hand in by smashing a mirror in the ship's bar. Once arrived, she embarked on a lecture tour before audiences that ranged from polite to thoroughly hostile. She was arrested for wrecking a pub in Newcastle-on-Tyne. In London she was again arrested, this time for breaking out a subway window with an umbrella. The offending pane contained a cigarette advertisement. British music hall audiences frequently treated her to showers of vegetables and rotten eggs. (Perhaps the British were insulted by her observation that fogs were God's way of punishing tobacco smokers.) She faced hostile crowds in Dublin, and was especially ill-received in Scotland. A Glasgow mob became so ugly that Nation was forced to duck for shelter into, of all places, a nearby hotel bar.

When she returned to America, Nation went into retirement on an Arkansas farm, although she found enough vim to smash her last saloon in Butte, Mt., on January 26, 1910. Early in 1911, she went to a hospital in Leavenworth, Ks., and remained there until she died on June 2 of that year. Death possibly came as a welcome relief; she had been arrested 30 times over the last 11 years of her life. Although she failed in her battle to destroy the liquor industry, she did eventually win the war, at least temporarily. Her high profile saloon smashing led to a stronger temperance movement, which in turn led to the passing of Prohibition from 1919 to 1933.

Carry Nation was buried in Belton, Mo. Her gravestone reads, "She hath done what she could." Many shell-shocked bartenders would have called that the all-time graveyard understatement.

William Van Dalsen

Murderer and Woodworker

A round eight o'clock in the long-forgotten evening of Monday, September 19, 1904, Frank Eckerle of Louisville was an agitated man. He was the proprietor of a saloon at 501 East Market Street, and he anticipated trouble with a customer. On the second floor were rooms that could be rented on a day-to-day basis. At a little past four in the afternoon, an attractive woman had rented a room and gone upstairs in the company of a young man. None of the groggery's employees or customers had seen or heard the couple leave, and it had been *awfully* quiet up there, and it was beginning to look inappropriate since occupants of the rooms were instructed to be out by seven p.m. Eckerle thought it his duty to investigate and throw the young visitor out of the building if anything unseemly had been going on. He marched up the stairs and knocked on the door, perhaps gently, as a subtle warning to cease any clandestine activities. No answer. Another knock— more insistent this time. Again, silence was the only response. Eckerle, fed up, pushed the unlocked door open. It was dark in the room, so he struck a match.

As it turned out, something unseemly *had* been going on in the rented room. The quarters were tiny, furnished only with a bed, washstand and basin, dressing table and stove, but the smallness of the room only added to the horror of the scene, as quantities of blood had been splashed throughout, particularly on the bed. The female occupant's body was leaning against the foot of the bed in a kneeling position, as if she had been praying at the moment of her violent death. Her upper half rested on the bed, her head on her left arm, the other arm thrown over her face; judging by the dried and clotted blood, she had been dead at least two hours. She was fully clothed save for her hat, found lying alone and newly ownerless on a dressing table. She had clearly fought her assailant, for her right arm was scratched and bore bruises in the shape of three fingers. A button had fallen off her dress in the scuffle. The cause of the woman's demise was soon apparent, even without the expertise of the coroner: her throat had been slashed ear to ear. In fact, she nearly had been decapitated.

Eckerle, understandably not eager to take in the view, ran downstairs calling for help. Bartender Tom Cavanaugh rushed up into the room and was sickened by the sight of the eight-inch gash in the

Fannie Porter. From the Louisville *Courier-Journal* of January 19, 1906.
Courtesy Courier-Journal.

woman's throat. The police and an undertaker were hastily summoned, and a crowd of gawkers was permitted to enter the bloody chamber and see the body, in hopes that one could positively identify her. Someone finally did: a man named Joe Busch recognized her as a local married woman named Fannie Dalton Porter, originally of West Virginia, aged about twenty-five. She had been separated from her husband John Porter for quite some time, after which she led a "wild life." It was said she had been involved with a number of men, and that she had a nine-year-old son who lived in Evansville, In.

The authorities searched the room and found no obvious trace of the murderer or his weapon. A bloody basin revealed that he had taken care to wash his hands. The ghastly deed had been done in utter silence; the bartender swore he heard no screams or struggling. The killer had managed to slip out of the saloon/apartment building undetected.

For all the murderer's stealth, it did not take long for the police to identify a suspect. Persons who knew Fannie Porter said the young man was probably William Van Dalsen, who had been Porter's boyfriend for several months and who had been living with her before she broke off the relationship. One of his coworkers at O.H. Kramer's carpentry firm stepped forward to reveal that he had seen Van Dalsen the day before the murder, and the latter said he wouldn't make it to work the next day. In addition, the police found witnesses who saw Porter and Van Dalsen together the afternoon of the murder.

A friend of the dead woman's named Hugh McKeown gave to the police a letter she had entrusted to him. It was from Van Dalsen, and could hardly have been more incriminating. It was an unsettling mixture of tenderness, pathos and murderous threats:

Louisville, Ky., Sept. 5, 1904. —Dear, Dear Fannie: I am down in the heart to write and see what in the world I can do to get you back again. You know I love you with all my heart and soul. The tears blind me so that I cannot write. I will do the right thing, and that you may know. You will have a nice home before cold weather sets in and won't have to run around. I will get Charley [her son, presumably] out for you inside of one month and keep him with us and send him to school, so he can make something out of himself when he gets big. I think you did me wrong by not leav-

Murderer and Woodworker

William Van Dalsen, murderer of Fannie Porter. From the Louisville *Courier-Journal* of January 19, 1906.

Courtesy Courier-Journal.

ing me a note or something to let me know why you left me suddenly. I am so sorry that it happened, but I will say that if you don't come back to me that I will fix you so you can never live with another man. I will give you till Saturday to decide and answer. If not, I will quit my job and hunt you down and kill you and that other man, and then fix myself... If you return to me before Saturday, I won't harm you. You told Louis Peterman that you would like to have a talk with me. You can see me at any old time or any old place you mention, for I am at your service and bothered so.

At this point in the letter, Van Dalsen dropped a strong hint that Porter had too much knowledge of his past for her own good:

You can get some money from me Saturday, or if you need it before, I will get it from Kramer for you, but don't think I am fool enough to let you run loose and know all that you know of me. When I told you of those things I thought we would be together all the time and placed confidence in you and told you all I know. I know that it ain't wise to put this in a letter but I don't care what comes of me now. I close for this time. Yours as ever, Will Van Dalsen, 706 Preston Street, care of O.H. Kramer. Good-bye

Fannie dear. With many kisses all for you. Don't laugh at this, for I am so worried and lonesome and heartbroken without you.

The police, considering this letter a pretty decent clue, organized a search for Van Dalsen. They didn't find him, but they did turn up some interesting testimony from one John Dolan, who had ridden in a streetcar with Porter Saturday morning, just two days before her death. Dolan was a stranger to Porter, but she was very talkative and seemed insistent on discussing her personal life. "I may be in trouble tomorrow. I may get in jail," she told him. "I intend to sue my husband for divorce and alimony."

"Aren't you afraid he will croak you?" Dolan asked, rather tactlessly.

Her reply was fatalistic: "Don't care if he does. Wish I was dead now." She also made a point of mentioning that she was living at Brook and Walnut Streets with her "fellow," not referring to her long-discarded husband. She may well have meant she was about to divorce Van Dalsen, who would later tell his aunt the two secretly had been married in West Virginia on October 15, 1903.

The police also discovered by questioning Porter's acquaintances that she had been afraid of her ex-boyfriend. She had told several friends she believed he would some day kill her, and many witnesses had heard him threatening to cut her throat. The consensus was that he was insanely jealous over her. One especially impressive witness was Mrs. James Sadler of 723 Franklin Street, who happened to be Porter's sister. Sadler confirmed the detectives' suspicion that Porter had dangerous knowledge of her lover's past.

"She told me just a few days ago that if she thought the police would get him before he got her, she would tell something that would send him where he could not molest her. I told sister if she was afraid of him, and believed he would kill her, that the best thing to do— the best way to get rid of him was to turn him up. I tried to get her to tell me what she knew, but she said she could not do it, but that it would send him to the gallows or the penitentiary for life."

A physical description of the suspect was sent out to all officers. Van Dalsen was twenty-eight years old, tall (5'11") and thin with black hair, had a couple of upper teeth missing and was invariably accompanied by his pet dog. Two Louisville detectives watched Van Dalsen's apartment building all night, but he did not show up. Nevertheless, the hard work paid off when at four in the afternoon of September 20, the day after the killing, the murderer was found hiding out in the home of his uncle W. Scott Van Dalsen, in New Albany, In. When the police arrived the killer was swinging nonchalantly in a hammock, smoking a cigarette and reading a newspaper account of his own crime. Glancing up at the arresting officers, he quietly remarked "I have been expecting you fellows all day." The bloody razor was still in his pocket, and on his person they also found a blood-stained shirt. He was arrested without incident and charged with the murder of Fannie Porter.

Back in Louisville, the police received their first of many hints that Van Dalsen was no ordinary murderer who denies all and then, when cornered, tearfully admits guilt and begs for mercy and forgiveness. Van Dalsen confessed eagerly, in such a matter-of-fact and emotionless manner "as he would have detailed a common-place story of an everyday occurrence" that the rattled press, which clearly had no idea what to make of him, called Van Dalsen "unfeeling and brutal" and a fiend. The killer revealed that once in the rented room with Porter, the couple drank considerable amounts of whisky, though they had already stopped at several saloons for drinks before they arrived at Eckerle's. The pair discussed their relationship, and Van Dalsen was overcome with jealousy after Porter told him she wanted to move from Louisville to Mason County, W. V.. The heavy drinking further clouded his judgment. Rather than have her leave and find someone else, Van Dalsen thought it better to detach her head from her body with a straight razor. Yet he had the audacity to claim she approved of the plan, despite the defensive wounds on her arm. As he told the story:

"I loved the woman and I did not want her to go away from me, and I told her so. I told her how I cared for her and that if she left I thought she would be treating me bad after all I had done for her—after she had spent my money so long. She commenced crying and said she loved me too, and then got a razor out of her stocking. I was drinking and did not pay much attention to the razor. I asked her to give it to me, and took it out of her hand. She told me to cut her throat, and I had a notion to do it then, but I talked with her some more about our life together, and laid the razor down. We talked on for a while— I don't know how long, but it was getting dark outside. I had my arms around her, when I saw the razor again. I said something else about cutting her throat, and she threw her head back and said 'Cut it.' I then got the razor and opened it and put my left arm around her neck. She looked at me and held her head back and said 'Cut my throat, Will.' I then pulled the razor across her throat." Most gruesomely, Van Dalsen would later claim he slit Porter's throat as she attempted to kiss him.

He continued his confession: "When I cut her throat, I think we were sitting on the edge of the bed— I was drunk and don't know exactly. When I pulled the razor across her throat the blood went in my coat sleeve and all over me. After she was cut she got up and I shoved her down on the floor. I then went to the washstand and washed my hands and my coat. I laid the razor down on the washstand, and when I had cleaned my coat I picked it up and washed it. I put it in my pocket and walked out of the building the way I went in— through the saloon."

(This last detail was not true. A bloody trail indicated the killer escaped by climbing over a railing and then down a flight of outside stairs. In addition, had he left by the saloon's door, the bartender would have heard an electric bell placed there to alert him when a customer entered or exited. Therefore, the police beheld the puzzling spectacle of a man who was willing to confess he had committed a horrible murder, but not willing to admit how he sneaked out of a building.)

Van Dalsen claimed that after the murder he visited several more saloons and partook of strong spirits. He also stopped at a restaurant on Jefferson Street and indulged in a hearty meal. At nine p.m., about three hours after the killing, he hopped a railroad car to New Albany, where he hid out until arrested. While confessing, Van Dalsen showed little emotion and seemed peculiarly unconcerned about his fate. This strange apathy was to become even more pronounced and remarkable in the months ahead.

To take Van Dalsen's confession at face value, he killed Porter simply out of jealousy. But detectives, remembering the threatening letter he sent her and the testimony of the late woman's sister, believed he had more than one motive to commit murder. It seemed obvious there was something in his past, possibly a major crime, that he was trying to keep hidden. Under pressure, Van Dalsen admitted he had deserted from the Navy several months previously. But this seemed hardly serious enough to "send him to the gallows or the penitentiary for life," as Porter's sister stated. The police decided to dig deeper into the killer's history.

A Mrs. Belle Cherry told detectives that the murdered woman used to date her son, and that Porter once confided to her that Van Dalsen killed an unnamed man "not so very far from here." The tale was corroborated by Mrs. John Brudley, acquaintance of both victim and murderer. She heard Porter make a cryptic remark hinting that Van Dalsen had killed before and would do so again. A friend of Van Dalsen's named James Burk stepped forward to reveal that in 1902 Van Dalsen told him he had indeed "killed a man, and it was not a hundred miles away either." When Burk pressed for details, Van Dalsen responded "If I tell you, you will know as much about it as I do." Burk told police he believed Van Dalsen had killed a stranger named Robert Blair, who also went by the aliases James Dorsey and James Clark. In 1899 or 1900, Blair had been found in the weeds of a vacant lot near Fulton and Shelby Streets dying of a fatal gunshot wound. He passed away two days later in the City Hospital without revealing the name of his murderer, saying to police "That is my business." The case had been classified as unsolved.

Encouraged, the police grilled Van Dalsen concerning the murder of Blair. He denied guilt but admitted he lived in the neighborhood when the crime occurred. Police dropped him as a suspect when they found in their files a note from an Ohio penitentiary claiming that a prisoner named Mooney confessed on his deathbed that he had shot a man in that area at that particular time.

Meanwhile, the press uncovered some unpleasant details about Van Dalsen's life. His mother had once run a house of ill fame on Fifth and Green Streets. When he was eight years old William and his two sisters were taken from their mother and placed in the School of Reform. The sisters eventually left the institution (one committed suicide in 1901), but Van Dalsen remained in the school until he was 21. Their mother had long since moved to Indianapolis, where she died only a few months before Van Dalsen killed Porter. As if all this weren't juicy enough, another letter turned up written from Van Dalsen to his victim. This one was written on Monday, the day of the murder. It read:

Dear Fannie: I sit down in tears and beg you to let me know where you are staying and why you do not want to live with me. I love you and you know it, and I tried to begin to do right and have something. I care for nothing in the world but you, and if I can't have you I will kill myself and be done with it. I never slept all night, so I am tired, sleepy, and disgusted with life. As I go to work this morning, I hope and pray you will answer this note and do right. I don't know what to say. I will close, hoping to find you well and happy. Yours as ever, William Van Dalsen.

From his prison cell on Murderer's Row, Van Dalsen awaited his trial, undoubtedly aware that a guilty verdict was a foregone conclusion and there was a noose looming in his future. Reporters who visited him were taken aback by his nearly complete lack of emotion. "I'm in it for good," he told one member of the press, "And I'll take my medicine." But still he insisted that the crime of which he hinted in the September 5 letter to Porter was simply that of military desertion, and that Porter was the only person he had ever murdered. Van Dalsen, who seems to have had quite a penchant for letter-writing, composed an open letter in his cell on the night of September 22, to be reproduced in the press. It was a masterpiece of death row bravado:

I am awaiting the finish just as happy as a man at the track watches his horse coming in the stretch and under the wire. At first the time passed slow for me, with little to eat and plenty to smoke and some men I knew on the outside. So I pass the time with cigarettes, for some one was kind enough to send them in to me. I give thanks to any that sent them to me, as I enjoy a good smoke. I will write a better letter some other time, for I can't get my mind on what I am doing. I had drunk enough whisky to float a steamboat in the last two weeks and had to stop so quick it was just like a hard fall to me, and I have not got over it yet. I go to court in the morning and I will waive the examination of the trial. It is a hard thing to think of, for a man who was never in jail before and to be here on a charge like this. The men here are not like a lot of rubes and try to jar any memory of what I have done.

Curiously, despite his impending trial for an atrocious murder, what really seemed to annoy Van Dalsen was a matter most would find trivial:

> *This morning the part of the jail where I was turned from a card game into a Sunday-school by the Sisters, who read some very nice stories and talked to us on a good subject. I was afraid they would get after me or ask to see me, for I am always being called to the gate for some one to take a pike [look] at me, and some people come and try to tell me that they know me, when they never saw me before.*

Van Dalsen was as good as his word when he was examined by the court on Friday, September 23. He refused to hire an attorney and he refused to make a statement other than "I have nothing to say, Your Honor." He seemed to care not at all when informed he was being held without bond. Despite the prisoner's wish to waive the examination, witnesses for the Commonwealth were called to the stand. These included poor Frank Eckerle, who recounted the fright he received when he first struck the match in that tiny rented room; bartender Cavanaugh, who positively identified Van Dalsen as the young man who accompanied Porter to her room; Ellen Harper, a friend of Porter's who knew of Van Dalsen's threats against the victim; and Herman Weist, an acquaintance of Van Dalsen's. Weist told the court that on the morning of the murder, Van Dalsen said to him "Herman, if Kramer [their boss] asks for me tomorrow, tell him to read the papers." This implied, contrary to Van Dalsen's confession, that the murder was a pre-meditated act.

After the hearing, which decidedly did not go in Van Dalsen's favor, the prisoner was led back to his cell "in his usual unconcerned, cheerful mood." He explained to a *Louisville Times* reporter about a month later, on October 21, "I was tired of lying in jail and wanted to have this thing over with one way or another." When the reporter asked why he had been so quick to plead guilty, Van Dalsen replied "Well, I did it. What else was there for me to do but plead guilty when I killed her?"

"But did you realize what they might do with you for this?"

"I don't give a damn what they do," said Van Dalsen. Then he laughed and lit a cigarette.

His demeanor did not change at his criminal trial, held on

November 21, 1904. The jury returned a guilty verdict after deliberating for slightly over an hour and he was sentenced to hang by the neck until dead. Although at the trial Van Dalsen repudiated his confession and claimed he had acted in self-defense, he was indifferent after the verdict was read.

"Well, they gave me the rope," he announced to his fellow inmates. "That was what I expected." The *Louisville Times* noticed that he delivered this statement "almost proudly." The time of execution was determined to be at dawn on January 19, 1906, giving him slightly more than a year to live. He continued to be held in the Jefferson County jail.

Many expected Van Dalsen to finally crack and show some concern for his fate. He never did. To the contrary, he seemed to become only more cheerful and unconcerned. Around Christmas 1905, the nation's papers were abuzz with wire reports concerning the condemned man's disturbing new hobby. After several weeks' labor, he had carved a miniature toy gallows out of wood. (Unanswered question: what jailhouse authority allowed a condemned murderer on death row free access to a pocket knife?) To add verisimilitude Van Dalsen also

carved a small hapless man, who resembled himself, out of a bar of soap. The wee fellow stood on the trapdoor with a string around his neck. The other end of the string was secured to a miniature crossbeam. ("If I just had a black cap to draw over this dummy's head, it would seem more realistic," Van Dalsen was heard to remark.) On his cell door the prisoner placed a sign that read "Drop a nickel in the slot and see the man drop." Sporting persons who did so found that inserting a five-cent piece activated a mechanical device that sprung the trap door, causing the soap man to do a sprightly mid-air jig while dangling from the string. "Nearly every visitor who calls at the jail puts in a nickel," according to the *Los Angeles Times*.

Van Dalsen was perhaps the only prisoner in history ever to be hanged in effigy, not by a mob, but by himself. He seemed grotesquely eager to please the customers: "Quite a number of people have paid for the privilege of witnessing a fake hanging today. Of course, they were deprived of the gurgling sound that generally goes with a hanging and there were other 'trimmings' that go with a genuine execution which they failed to see, but all got their nickel's worth. When I'm shot through the trap on the morning of January 19, I guess the appetite of those who wish to witness such things will be satisfied. I gave them the best I had in the shop today, but I will give them all the 'trimmings' then."

A reporter asked Van Dalsen where he got the notion for such a device. The prisoner laughed and pointed to his forehead: "I'm full of good ideas. I really need the money and didn't know just how else to get it. Most everybody likes to witness a hanging and why shouldn't I gratify their curiosity by giving them a fake exhibition before the real thing occurs? I can profit by this, and I can't by the other." He refused to say how much money he made from his enterprise, for fear of making his fellow prisoners jealous. The reporter could not keep from commenting, "He seems to have lost all human instinct and revels in making other people's blood creep." Their flesh too, no doubt.

There was talk that Van Dalsen's execution might be delayed by legal technicalities, but this proved to be only talk. Excitement ran high as the day drew closer— ran high for everyone except Van Dalsen, who still appeared as unconcerned as if he knew he had 100 years yet to live.

On January 17, two days before the scheduled hanging, he was visited in jail by a pretty local girl, 18-year-old Miss Ethel Gentry, along with two of her girlfriends. Gentry, moved by the condemned man's plight, melodramatically offered to kiss him between the iron bars. Van Dalsen bashfully refused, but after his visitor left the building admitted he turned her down only because he didn't want to be teased by the guards.

Nevertheless, he wrote a note to the young woman and had it delivered to her home at 523 Marshall Street. She returned to the jail at eight o'clock on the morning of the 18th, fewer than 24 hours before Van Dalsen was to be hanged. They had a quiet conversation— exactly about what, we will never know— then she left again, promising to return. As she was leaving an interested party asked Gentry if she were Van Dalsen's sweetheart.

"No, I am not," she replied. "I just feel sorry for him. I knew him before he got into this trouble, and I liked him." She vaguely commented that they had been discussing the "trouble" he had gotten himself into.

The public wondered if Van Dalsen's notorious calm exterior would ever crack and snapped up newspapers to read every detail of his behavior as he entered the valley of the shadow of death. The *Courier-Journal* of January 18 asked the question: "Will Van Dalsen's nerve remain with him to the last? That is the question that is agitating the minds of all who have seen him. There are those who think that before the black cap is slipped over his head he will lose his unconcern and plead for mercy. Others are of the opinion that his cool bearing will remain with him to the end, and that he will show no sign of fear when he ascends the scaffold."

Those who held the latter opinion were correct. Just hours before the end, Van Dalsen occupied his time looking calmly out the window of his cell at all the free people walking on Green Street, "cooler than those about him." At one point during his final day he asked to see the scaffold, and permission was granted. The trap was sprung for his benefit, and he remarked "My, what a lot of noise it makes. Will my feet touch the ground?" He laughed at his own joke.

During that evening of January 18, the prisoner's lady caller Ethel Gentry returned as promised. She wept so much that she had to be escorted from the building. Van Dalsen sat unmoved.

The evening of January 18 came and went, bearing no reprieve. Van Dalsen was certainly to be hanged in the yard of the Jefferson County Jail the next morning at sunrise, just a little after 7 a.m. The prisoner received this news around nine p.m. His only response was to puff on a cigar. Around 9:30 he ended the last discussion with his two court-appointed lawyers, Edward Bloomfield and William A. Perry. Van Dalsen ate his final supper around ten o'clock, with little or no comment. Shortly afterward he stretched out on his cot and "slept as quietly and peacefully as a baby."

When he woke around 4:10 a.m., Deputy Shupp asked how he felt.

"All right, I guess. The only thing I hate is passing through the crowd and saying goodbye as I go to the scaffold."

Someone else asked if he had slept well. "Sure, slept all right."

"Did you have any dreams?"

"No, no dreams. I never dream."

One of the men present offered Van Dalsen a cigar after breakfast. "Better give it to me now. I may not see you again."

Someone with a philosophical bent asked "Where are you going, Van?"

"I don't know until I get there."

Shortly after sunrise on the morning of January 19, 1906, Van Dalsen was led to the scaffold, "placidly indifferent, his eyes wearing the same quizzical look with which he always gazed at strangers, showing no realization of what it all meant." Hundreds had come to see him hanged: the jail yard was full, and spectators were staring out of neighboring windows and from rooftops. Two hundred men and boys stood on the roof of the Armory building alone. Some even precariously climbed telephone poles in order to get a good look. However, there was no carnival atmosphere. The crowd was somber and silent. It was remarked more than once that the condemned man was the only truly calm person present. Van Dalsen walked through the throng with his head up, gazing into the faces in the crowd as if he were simply going before a school assembly to pick up a diploma. When he recognized someone in the crowd, he smiled.

One person in the crowd was very glad to see Van Dalsen there: Mrs. James Sadler, sister of Fannie Porter. She was accompanied by Charles Ratcliffe, the first of Porter's multiple husbands. Watching from behind a thick glass window only about six feet away from the gallows, Sadler was infuriated that the killer could be so serene under the circumstances. Sounding very much like a heroine from a turn-of-the-century novel, she shouted at Van Dalsen "Shiver, you brute! You die like a chicken!"

Nevertheless, Van Dalsen showed no concern for himself. As he stood on the trap door the black hood was placed over his head, and then the rope around his neck. Deputy Sheriff Frank Carroll adjusted the noose and said "May God have mercy on you." Van Dalsen audibly whispered "Goodbye." The trap was sprung at 7:24 a.m., but Van Dalsen's exit from the world was not without its moment of black comedy. Carroll had unwittingly been standing on the trap door along with the prisoner, and only a deputy's lightning-fast reflexes prevented Carroll from tumbling through space along with the condemned man.

Whatever humor the incident may have inspired vanished within seconds. Van Dalsen jerked spasmodically in mid-air, fingers twitching and body swaying. Fifteen minutes later, when he was definitely dead, the body was examined by the attending physician, Dr. William Kellar. The knot had slipped, and it appeared that rather than having his neck instantaneously broken, Van Dalsen may have strangled to death.

The body was taken to the undertaking establishment of H. Bosse and Son, where it was coffined and displayed to over 1,000 spectators. One of them was Ethel Gentry, who wept copiously. Later in the afternoon, Van Dalsen's body was taken to the public vault at St. Michael's Cemetery. His funeral was attended by a few friends and no relatives. He remains there as forgotten as the woman he killed.

The nature of the other serious crime supposedly committed by Van Dalsen and alluded to in his letter to Fannie Porter of September 5, 1904, was never discovered. Also disappointingly, the record does not state whatever became of the pride and joy of Van Dalsen's final days, his homemade toy gallows.

Nathan B. Stubblefield

Inventor

"For of all sad words of tongue or pen/ The saddest are these: 'It might have been.'" So wrote poet John Greenleaf Whittier in 1856. It would be hard to find a better and more succinct description of the life of Nathan Stubblefield, a Kentucky farmer and inventor whose name, in a more just world, would be a household word today.

He was born in Murray, Calloway County, on December 27, 1860, to William J. and Victoria Stubblefield. It was apparent early on that he had little aptitude for schoolwork, and Nathan dropped out of school when he was 15. It was not a question of intellectual capability, for Stubblefield began a program of rigorous self-education, reading everything he could find about science and, in particular, electricity. In fact, the young man gradually became a good amateur electrician, and by 1887 he had made and patented several improvements in the telephone. He also held patents on a lamp lighter and an electric battery.

When not occupied with farming and inventing, Stubblefield dated a local girl named Ada May Buchanan. The couple married around 1881 and had 10 children, of whom six survived to adulthood. As Stubblefield continued his experiments with electricity, he developed a reputation as an eccentric. A reporter from St. Louis would write: "He is a recluse... His neighbors shun him, while they respect him. None ever intrudes upon his privacy— they know well that such intrusion means a rebuff long to be remembered. The little town of Murray is full of stories of his eccentricities, which, possibly, are the growth of not understanding a man whose ideals were far beyond those of the neighborhood.... He cares only for his home, his family, and— electricity."

The Italian physicist Guglielmo Marconi would later be given credit for the invention of the wireless radio, but many contrarians insist Nathan Stubblefield should rightly be called the Father of Radio. This claim is overstated, as will become evident, but Stubblefield might properly be called the father of the wireless telephone. His inventions paved the way for radio and other modern marvels as well.

By 1890, when Marconi was still a teenager, Stubblefield had already developed a wireless telephone. He demonstrated it at his farm in Murray to a few friends, who were startled to hear Stubblefield's voice issuing from a box though he stood far away. Strangely, he filed no patent on his invention.

Word got out, and soon enough the community was clamoring for a public demonstration of this magical concept of sending voices through the air without wires. Stubblefield obliged them in 1892. At the courthouse lawn in Murray, he set up two boxes about 200 feet apart. The boxes were two feet square and unconnected, and each contained a telephone. Stubblefield and his son were able to carry on a conversation from a distance without the aid of wires. According to the late

133

Inventor

journalist and commentator Frank Edwards (not often the most reliable of sources), instead of being impressed by the miracle they had just witnessed, the assembled crowd laughed at Stubblefield's presumption.

Whether or not the story of the crowd's reaction is true, it was another 10 years before Stubblefield again demonstrated his invention in public. An article in the *Louisville Courier-Journal* of December 26, 1901, listed by name several prominent citizens of Calloway County who signed an affidavit describing the "electrical achievements" they had witnessed on Stubblefield's farm, noting "His system is as yet unknown to the scientific world."

Perhaps encouraged by this report, the inventor decided to hold another experiment on the streets of Murray. On New Year's Day 1902, before a crowd of 1,000 people, Stubblefield once more set up boxes containing wireless telephones, but this time at a much greater distance. The inventor transmitted the voice of his son Bernard from the Stubblefield house to a shed, and then to a receiver roughly a mile away. Bernard also played harmonica and whistled some tunes for the crowd, making him the first musician ever to be heard via wireless. Persons at five listening stations along the route were "astounded at the remarkable success achieved," according to the *Courier-Journal* of January 3.

The two *Courier-Journal* articles contained some prescient comments by the inventor: "Mr. Stubblefield expects to see his invention adopted throughout the world within a short while. He says that the cost of establishing a system with his apparatus will be a mere trifle as compared with the cost of the system now in use."

News of this triumph spread widely and quickly. A reporter from the *St. Louis Post-Dispatch* contacted Stubblefield and asked for a demonstration, to which the inventor agreed. The correspondent was the first reporter to be allowed a close look at Stubblefield's workshop, and the inventor even allowed the paper to publish photos of himself demonstrating the wireless. The experiment took place at the farm on January 10, 1902, and was another success. The reporter clearly heard son Bernard's voice transmitted from a distance of 500 yards, and later from a mile. Nathan Stubblefield told the astonished newsman that someday it would be possible to hear weather reports, news and music from all over the world via wireless telephony. (Amusingly, the reporter also noted that the inventor hid electric wires in his watermelon patch in order to hear thieves raiding his produce in the dark of night.)

To put it in perspective, these experiments took place about a month after Marconi sent the single letter "S" in Morse code across the Atlantic. Stubblefield was transmitting voices and music while "Marconi himself could only send and receive dot and dash code," as Edwards put it. Of course, Marconi could transmit his signals much farther than Stubblefield, a fact that would be the latter's undoing.

Financiers became interested in Stubblefield's invention, and a few months later he traveled to Philadelphia for another successful public display. On March 20, 1902, he went to Washington, D.C., where he outdid himself by placing his transmitter on the steamship *Bartholdi* and his receiver on shore. This was the best attended and most well publicized of all his experiments, and once again Stubblefield emerged triumphant. The congressmen and dignitaries on land were able to communicate with passengers on the steamer. The *Washington Evening Star* of March 21 praised Stubblefield highly, proclaiming "Wireless Telephony Demonstrated Beyond Question."

At this point it must have seemed to Stubblefield that things were finally falling into place. No longer, it appeared, would he have to sell vegetables to support his family while tinkering with his machines. After years of toiling in obscurity he achieved every inventor's dream: recognition for his work and businessmen who wanted to develop his wireless telephone. And that is just when his life began falling apart.

Suspicious of others, Stubblefield decided to finance his invention himself. He formed the Wireless Telephone Company of America, incorporated on May 22, 1902. The major problem was that the inventor had no head for business. Rather than promote the product, the company engaged in selling stock, and little else. Only one of his wireless telephone systems was sold. The company folded, bankrupting Stubblefield.

Another problem was that he never officially patented his invention. It probably would not have mattered, in any case. Rapid advances in Marconi's wireless radio system rendered the Stubblefield system obsolete. (In 1908 he did patent a method for placing radios in automobiles, so Stubblefield might be called the father of the car radio, but he made no money from that invention, either.)

From there it was a downhill slide. Stubblefield retreated back into obscurity and became a bitter hermit. He and his wife divorced after their youngest child left home, and soon afterward his house burned down. In his dire poverty, Stubblefield proudly refused all offers of aid, even from his brother Walter. He continued working on inventions, but shortly before his death he destroyed all his creations and burned the blueprints.

He died alone on March 28, 1928, in his miserable shack where his body lay several days before it was discovered. Cause of death was starvation. He was buried in a pauper's unmarked grave in Murray.

Did Nathan Stubblefield actually "invent radio," as is often claimed? There remains some controversy on this point. He was the first to transmit and receive sound via airwaves, but his invention had a maximum range of only about eight miles, far less efficient than Marconi's method of transmitting sound. For that reason, it cannot be definitely stated that Stubblefield was the creator of radio broadcasting. However, he did invent the wireless telephone. In fact, the Stubblefield system is still being used today in museums as a communication system for the hearing impaired.

In May 1991, the Kentucky Broadcasters Association refused to adopt a resolution proclaiming Stubblefield the inventor of radio, choosing instead to note Stubblefield's "contribution to the early development of wireless transmissions." This infuriated at least one of the inventor's descendants, who claimed Stubblefield's system used the sophisticated principle of amplitude modulation (necessary to AM broadcasting), something the board denied.

But even if Nathan Stubblefield has been forgotten everywhere else, he is fondly remembered in the town of Murray. The local AM radio station's identification call letters spell out the inventor's initials: WNBS. In addition, the courthouse lawn features a stone monument marking the spot where, in 1902, Stubblefield made history— or, rather, should have.

John Shell

Old Man

It was surprising when John Shell died in Leslie County. It seemed to many as though he had been putting off that activity indefinitely, for Shell had been famous for his longevity. In fact, he had been billed for years as "The Oldest Man In The World," and it was alleged that at the time of his demise he was a couple of months short of his 134th birthday.

Facts about Shell's antecedents are murky at best. It was said that he had been born to Sam and Mary Ann Frye Shell on September 2, 1788. (Local legend has it that his mother was a midget.) Sources differ as to whether he was born in North Carolina or Tennessee; Shell claimed the former location as his place of birth in the 1850 census, and then claimed the latter in 1900. Nevertheless, most sources agree the family moved to Kentucky when he was supposedly around 12. The family lived first in Bell County, then Harlan and finally Leslie County. For a time Sam Shell operated a water mill at Poor Fork, near Baxter in Harlan County.

John Shell has been described by genealogist Sadie Wells Stidham as a jack of all trades. He worked at his father's water mill for a while, and records show that he hewed the logs to build the Harlan County courthouse in 1860. He also found work as a farmer, beekeeper, riflemaker, wood carver, blacksmith, and storekeeper. A couple of times a month Shell rode to Jonesville, Va., where he sold honey, herbs and his wood carvings. In addition, Shell kept up his father's tradition by building the first water mill in Leslie County near his home on Greasy Creek.

Shell's first wife was Elizabeth (Betsey) Nantz, whom he married in Harlan County on October 19, 1844. Because she was from Holland and spoke little or no English, Shell nicknamed her "Dutch." They dwelled at Greasy Creek in Clay (later Leslie) County in a house where Shell lived the rest of his life. This log house was of sturdy construction, with puncheon floors. There were two rooms upstairs and two down. Remarkably, the house was still standing as of 1975, when the Kentucky Historical Society named it a state shrine, along with another durable tiny log cabin Shell lived in while building his permanent house. At one time, the bigger house was still filled with Shell's memorabilia, including an old spinning wheel, mill barrels, a tool box, ox shoes, an old saddle, a wheat cradle and a long split board that Shell had intended to use in the construction of his own coffin.

John and Betsey Shell had 11 children: William, Nicholas, Polly, John P.M., Martha, Elizabeth, Abijah, McClellan, Emily, Mary Ann, and Bentley. As if that were not amazing enough, Betsey herself allegedly lived to the ripe old age of 112. After her death, Shell remained a widower 12 years. Then he married Betsy Chappell, who at 45 was far less than half of his alleged age. She bore Shell's youngest son, Albert, on February 27, 1915.

Word spread to other counties about the incredible age of "Uncle John," as he was known to the community, especially after the birth of Albert. The old man and his boy were a featured attraction at the 1919 Kentucky State Fair in Louisville, an idea conceived by the Board of Commerce. His train ride to Lexington and Louisville was the first one of his life. Dressed in his brand new blue jeans and sporting a long, flowing white beard, he looked exactly the way one might expect a 131-year-old mountaineer to look. He was five feet, five inches tall and weighed a little over 100 pounds. His eyesight was still so good that he could shoot a squirrel with a hunting rifle. In fact, Shell beat a 25-year-old grandson at a target shoot held on his farm in 1919. He was a moderate imbiber of whiskey and user of tobacco. He claimed to have cut a third set of teeth when he was well past 100.

He was the hit of the show as he charmed the crowd with anecdotes and the secrets of his longevity: "Hog, hominy, and honey," and "Hard work is the way to keep well." The crowd gave Shell $175 in quarters in his first half-day as he and his son sat out in the open air. The fair managers moved them into a tent, and thereafter Shell made another $700. The *Courier-Journal* induced him to take a ride in an airplane one day, and upon landing Shell expressed great enthusiasm, saying he would like to repeat the experience.

He didn't care much for his new clothes, though, and when the fair was over and he returned to Leslie County, Shell replaced the blue jeans with his old homemade linsey trousers. According to writer Mary Brewer, as late as 1963 his discarded old jacket still hung right where he last left it, on a nail in his old house. She wrote "On the lapel one could see the blue ribbon and button that he won at the State Fair, with only a hint of the blue still clinging to the fabric."

In 1920 the Kentucky Illiteracy Commission made an effort to teach Shell how to read and write. A teacher named Zilpha Roberts was sent to Greasy Creek, but she found Shell unable or unwilling to learn and living in squalor besides, with pigs wandering through his cabin. By then his second wife had also died and Shell lived completely alone much of the time. On occasion he was known to stay with some of his neighbors.

Physicians who examined Shell doubted that he was actually over 130 years old, but admitted he was possibly very close to 100. Nevertheless, his claim was treated with respect. When the elderly gentleman celebrated what he said was his 133rd birthday in 1921, the *New York Times* duly noted the occasion on page one.

Death finally came for Shell on July 6, 1922. Although he had never been seriously ill in his life, he fell and hurt his back while breaking in a horse. He succumbed to his injuries that night, calmly discussing his funeral arrangements as he lay dying. His passing received front page coverage in both the *Louisville Courier-Journal* and the *Lexington Herald*, complete with photos. The editorial writer at the *Herald* saw in Shell's life a lesson for everyone: if you would live long, work hard and live simply.

John Shell, the oldest man in the world? From the Lexington *Herald* of July 10, 1922.
Courtesy Herald-Leader.

Two of Shell's children attended his funeral. One was his eldest son, Will, age 75. The other was Will's younger half-brother Albert, who was seven years old.

Shell's gravestone proclaims to the world with solemn assurance that he was 134 years old when he died. When pressed for evidence concerning his age, Shell would claim he had a poll tax receipt in his name dated 1809. (A man did not legally have to pay a poll tax until he turned 21.) There were skeptics. The *Courier-Journal* suggested in an editorial after Shell's demise that "It would be unkind to examine too closely... [t]hat stained old receipt," but continued in a tongue-in-cheek vain. "To spend more than 100 years living the hard and isolated life of Greasy Creek certainly entitles Uncle Johnny to the resolution of all doubts in his favor." The *New York Times* ran a similar editorial, more condescending in tone.

Alas, the wonderful story of Shell's advanced age does not hold up under close inspection. In the 1880 Leslie County census, Shell gave his age as fifty-eight, which would mean he was actually born in 1822 rather than 1788. The 1900 census corroborates that John Shell of White Oak precinct was born in May (not September) 1822. In addition, the 1900 census reveals that Shell's first wife Betsey, who was allegedly 112 when she died, was almost exactly the same age as her husband. She was born in April 1822.

The conclusion is inescapable: unless Shell was fibbing about his age to the census takers and making himself seem *younger* than he actually was, he was really about 100 years old when he died. Writer James S. Greene II suggests that Shell, "lacking written records, lost track of his birthday and gradually stretched his age." Another possibility is that Shell simply enjoyed pulling people's legs concerning his real age. In any case, fathering a child at ninety-three and then reaching the century mark should be a proud achievement for any man.

Edgar Cayce

"Psychic"

One of the most offbeat of Kentuckians was born in Hopkinsville, Christian County, on March 18, 1877, a modest and mild-mannered young man who went on to become legendary as a psychic and healer.

If the biographers of Edgar Cayce (pronounced "Casey") are to be trusted, it was clear from his childhood that his life was going to be anything but ordinary. His paternal grandfather had been a water dowser of local fame, and Cayce claimed that as a small boy he communed with his grandfather's spirit after the latter's death, and that he was visited by an angel when he was 13. His mother, too, claimed the ability to speak with the invisible dead.

Cayce's father, Leslie, had been a justice of the peace and was known as Squire Cayce. As one might expect, he was a practical man who had no use for paranormal claims. He was irritated by his son's dreamy ways, especially when it developed that Cayce performed very poorly in school due to an inability to concentrate. One night his father threatened him with severe punishment if he failed to learn a list of words in a spelling textbook. Cayce was distraught at this prospect, but when his father stormed out of the room he heard a voice from an unseen source which told him "If you can sleep a little, we can help you." Cayce tried it and found that if he slept with the book (or any

Offbeat Kentuckians

other book) under his head, the entire contents would somehow become embedded permanently in his memory. Through this unorthodox means, his academic position at school improved exponentially—at least, to hear Cayce's biographers tell it.

The next big event in Cayce's life was an injury he received at school when another student struck him on the spinal cord with a baseball. Seemingly uninjured at first, the quiet child's behavior took an abrupt turnaround before the day was over. He became manic, shouting and picking fights with other students and even throwing himself before a team of horses. His worried parents put him to bed, and soon thereafter Cayce sank into a coma. But while still unconscious, legend has it, Cayce spoke to his parents, informing them of the nature of his injury, and adding that the cure was to make a poultice of herbs and chopped raw onions, which was then to be placed at the base of his

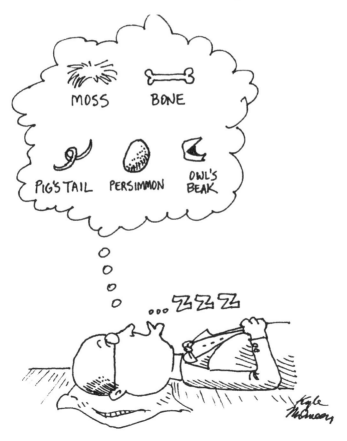

brain. The comatose boy added, "Hurry up, or there will be permanent damage to the brain." The astounded parents carried out Cayce's instructions to the letter, and he was miraculously healed.

As the story goes, when Cayce grew up his psychic powers developed in two ways: he discovered with the help of a hypnotist friend named Al Layne that he could slip into a trance and diagnose the source of a sick person's illness, even if that person was not present, and pre-scribe miracle cures made up of natural ingredients such as herbs and vegetables. In addition, he discovered that he had the gift of prophecy.

Naturally these astounding abilities made Cayce a much sought-after person, especially among relatives of ill persons whose cases had been given up as lost causes by established medical science. He soon acquired a sobriquet, the "Sleeping Prophet." Pro-Cayce writers claim his diagnoses and cures were almost always successful, but as we shall see, assertions of this nature concerning Cayce's talents should be taken with a grain of salt.

Cayce started out doing trance readings in Hopkinsville, find-ing himself in demand even after he moved to Bowling Green. His rep-utation quickly spread. Cayce, ever publicity-shy, wanted to live as nor-mal a life as possible. He got a job as a clerk in a Bowling Green book-store and married his sweetheart, Gertrude Evans, but his fame as a psy-chic and trance healer grew to the point where he was inundated with requests from the desperate all across the country, especially after the prestigious *New York Times* ran a feature story about him in 1910. Cayce, eager to provide help for those who needed it, would get letters begging for his aid, then literally sleep on the problem. Those who tran-scribed his cures as he talked in his sleep claimed that when in a trance, he always started off his diagnoses with the phrase "Yes, we have the body." He never accepted more than $25 for his services, and in fact often did his readings for free. He supported his family via several occu-pations throughout his life, working at various times as a clerk in a dry goods store and a bank, a salesman of both insurance and stationery and a professional photographer.

When Cayce died on January 3, 1945, he left behind a legacy of 30,000 case histories still filed away at the Association for Research and Enlightenment, built for that purpose in Virginia Beach, Va.

Offbeat Kentuckians

An obvious question must be answered: was Cayce actually psychic?

While no one can answer with a positive yes or no, it appears that he was not. Cayce seems to have been a sincere man who genuinely believed he was blessed with paranormal powers that he could use to benefit mankind. This touching desire to help others was one of Cayce's best features, and it elevates him into something of a tragic figure. It is his followers who engage in outright exaggeration, sometimes to sell books, sometimes simply to boost the master's reputation.

As with fellow psychics Nostradamus and Jeane Dixon, Cayce's supporters concentrate only on his few successes, and either ignore or rationalize his scores of misses. For instance, he prescribed cures occasionally for patients who, unbeknownst to him, were already dead.

An objective examination of Cayce's "psychic" medical diagnoses yields interesting results. Most of the letters sent to him by trusting patients have been preserved, and the majority of the writers described their symptoms in detail. In other words, the information was *given to him* by the patients themselves. Several examples of such letters to Cayce are reproduced in a biography by Thomas Sugrue entitled *There Is A River*. It seems Cayce did not use mystical mental processes to divine medical ailments, other than occasional guesswork when his correspondents weren't detailed enough. Anyone with a rudimentary knowledge of medicine could then lift an appropriately quaint remedy from a home medical encyclopedia. Not surprisingly, Cayce's psychic prescriptions are often very similar to folk remedies found in any number of reference guides from the period. For example, he prescribed oil of smoke for leg sores, peach-tree poultice for convulsions, bedbug juice for dropsy, and fumes of apple brandy from a charred keg for tuberculosis. He also prescribed laetrile for cancer. This substance contains cyanide, and is "known to be ineffective for cancer," according to skeptic Robert Todd Carroll.

It is also apparent to the casual reader that when making a diagnosis, Cayce was careful to mention as many organs and anatomical landmarks as possible, obviously in hopes that if he cast a large enough net, he would get a "hit." When his own wife was ailing, Cayce's reading was ".... from the head, pains along through the body from the second, fifth, and sixth dorsals, and from the first and second lumbar... tie-ups here, floating lesions, or lateral lesions, in the muscular and nerve fibers which supply the lower end of the lung and the diaphragm... in conjunction with the sympathetic nerve of the solar plexus, coming in conjunction with the solar plexus at the end of the stomach...."

It may sound detailed and precise, but upon closer inspection it is so vague that Cayce has covered most of the human body! In fact, Mrs. Cayce had tuberculosis. The Sleeping Prophet's followers consider this a "hit" because he happened to mention the lung. But they conveniently overlook the fact that he mentioned the head, three dorsals, two lumbars, muscular fibers, the nerves, the diaphragm, the solar plexus and the stomach, as well.

But what about the people who apparently took Cayce's advice and got better? They could have been cured by the power of suggestion (placebos *do* often work, after all). And, as skeptic James Randi points out, many illnesses are psychosomatic or self-terminating. Hence, there is little doubt many patients got better on their own and naively gave Cayce and his wild root soup all the credit. And perhaps sometimes the folk remedies actually worked, as they would have even without all the mystical trimmings.

Cayce's reputation has also been well served by his followers' tendency to exaggerate certain details of his life while negating others. For example, pro-Cayce literature often notes that one of his earliest champions was a doctor named Wesley H. Ketchum. This makes it sound as though at least some mainstream physicians believed in Cayce's abilities. What is often not mentioned is that Ketchum was a homeopathic, rather than an orthodox, physician. Ketchum himself has gone on record complaining that mainstream medical science refused to take the Sleeping Prophet seriously.

Then there is the 1910 *New York Times* article that, more than anything else, sparked Cayce's national reputation. The headline was "Illiterate Man Becomes A Doctor When Hypnotized," complete with lurid illustrations. The piece contains a detailed biography of Cayce and quotes from one of Ketchum's lectures (at one point the doctor compares Edgar Cayce none too subtly to Jesus Christ). But there are contradictions between the article and the established Cayce legend: how could he have been illiterate if he had merely to sleep on a book to absorb all its information? How did he make outstanding grades as a schoolboy with such a handicap? If Cayce had been illiterate, how could he have worked as a clerk in a bookstore? Did others have to read to him the letters he received from the desperately ill? How did he manage to compose hundreds of notes, predictions and letters to his patients? Clearly, Cayce was indeed literate, but this has been downplayed because his feats become less impressive if one realizes he was perfectly capable of reading and memorizing information in medical handbooks.

The *Times*'s early profile of Cayce is equally interesting for what it doesn't include. There is no mention of Cayce's having been visited by an angel at the age of 13, a story that crops up in later biographies. It does not mention the detail about his gaining knowledge as a child by sleeping with books under his head. It more modestly claims that after a nap, Cayce could remember better whatever he had studied before sleeping. (In other words, Cayce's memory improved after he got sufficient rest. Some psychic breakthrough.) Nor does the article bring up Cayce's first trance reading, during which he dramatically cured himself after being struck in the spine with a baseball. And yet all of these details appear in a biography written by Thomas Sugrue, a friend of Cayce's, and first published in 1942, three years before the psychic died. A logical conclusion is that many of the astounding "facts" in the life of Cayce were fabricated after 1910 to make the story better.

So much for the medical diagnoses. What of Cayce's predictions for the future, of which he made hundreds? (The higher the number of scattershot predictions a "psychic" makes, the better the odds that at least some of them will come true. This is what has kept up Nostradamus' reputation for over 400 years.) Upon even a cursory examination of Cayce's predictions, it is obvious that the most remarkable aspect of his writing is its utter evasiveness and haphazard wording. This is another common trick among clairvoyants: if predictions are worded vaguely, they can be made to apply to almost any event— after the fact, of course. Ambiguity is the prognosticator's best friend, since believers are sure to find meanings that were never there to begin with.

This certainly holds true for Cayce. Here is a handsome example of the Sleeping Prophet's syntax, as quoted by James Randi. Cayce is trying to explain away one of his predictions which proved incorrect: "...if the proper consideration is given all facts and factors concerning each character of information sought, as has been given oft, the information answers that which is sought at the time in relationships to the conditions that exist in those forms through which the impressions are made for tangibility or for observation in the minds of others."

Nearly all of Cayce's prose sounds like that. He also fills his diagnoses and predictions with qualifying phases such as "perhaps," and "I feel that...," just in case they don't come to pass. Rarely does he say anything concisely and clearly. In the final analysis, as with Nostradamus, Cayce's predictions work fine when applied to events after they occur, but they are completely useless as accurate predictors of the future. Perhaps one should think of them as postdictions rather than predictions.

Then there are the scores of Cayce predictions for the future, as opposed to medical diagnoses, that simply did not come true. For example, during the Great Depression he predicted 1933 would be a strong financial year. He predicted that in 1958 America would discover a death ray responsible for the destruction of Atlantis. He foretold that China would become a Christian nation and that Atlantis would rise, both by 1968. Here are a few of his prognostications that his followers claimed would come to pass by 1999: New York City will be destroyed, as will large portions of the Eastern states, "probably in the 1990s." But California and most of the Western states will be demolished "long before" the above happens. (Notice Cayce does not explain how such deeply unlikely phenomena will occur.) Japan will disappear into the sea. Northern Europe will "vanish suddenly." Starvation and suffering will become a rarity in India. American politics will become more stable; political influence groups will lose their power.

Faced with all of these failed predictions and logical explanations for his feats, there is no compelling reason to believe Cayce had the ability either to make long-distance medical diagnoses or read the future. In the end, we are left with a well-meaning, kindly man who was convinced he had special mental powers, and was able to encourage others to believe it as well. It cannot be said that he did anyone harm, nor can it be said that he did much good.

Death Valley Scotty

Prospector

The tourist in Death Valley, Ca., hasn't much lush scenery to enjoy. It is the kind of place that sets unpleasant records: the heart of the valley contains the lowest land in the Western hemisphere (282 feet below sea level), and in 1913 the highest temperature ever recorded in the United States was observed there (134 degrees Fahrenheit). It is also the driest place north of the equator, averaging two inches of rain per year. Explorers who are able to contend with the punishing heat and arid conditions are treated to vast expanses of forbidding desert with scant vegetation but ample amounts of borax.

Death Valley does contain one unexpected show place to attract tourists. In the far northern section of the desert, in the blowing sand and rocky terrain of Grapevine Canyon, stands an elegant mansion as out of place as a cathedral in the center of the ocean. It is Death Valley Ranch, more commonly known as Scotty's Castle, in honor of the prospector for whom it was constructed: Walter Scott, a longtime resident of one of the most inhospitable places on earth who became a living legend under the nickname Death Valley Scotty.

He was a Kentuckian, born in Cynthiana, Harrison County, probably on September 20, 1872, but this is uncertain because no birth record has ever turned up. Scotty himself was no help, as he claimed different birthdates that ranged over a period of several years. Strict adherence to the truth was not a trait that encumbered Scotty's story-telling. His parents were George and Anna Scott, and he was the youngest of six children.

Scotty's older brothers traveled west and became ranch hands. Scotty left home to join his brothers Bill and Warner when he was about 14 years old (later Scotty alleged he struck out on his own when only eight). Gradually he worked as a cowboy in Wells, Nv., for John Sparks, later to become the state's governor.

He became skillful at riding and roping, and around 1888 he was employed by Buffalo Bill Cody's traveling Wild West Show as a sharpshooter and stunt rider. Scotty would later claim to have per-formed before the crowned heads of Europe and to have been given a cigar by the King of Spain. Whether he hobnobbed with monarchs is a matter of conjecture, but it is certain that he spent considerable time learning the art of promotion from Cody's publicity man, Major Burke. (Revealingly, in his later years Scotty kept a framed picture of P.T. Barnum on his dresser.) Ever thirsty for fame and wealth, Scotty would return west and prospect for gold during the show's winter off-season.

In 1900, two major events occurred in Scotty's life: he got a job working in a Colorado gold mine, and in November he married a New York candy store clerk named Ella McCarthy in Cincinnati. He first introduced himself to her by tossing his cowboy hat across the store; it landed in a pile of fresh caramels. Scotty's superintendent at the mine gave the new bride a gift of two large pieces of gold ore. This planted an idea in Scotty's scheming mind.

A few years after leaving Buffalo Bill's show, he made Death Valley his place of residence. His first experience in that region occurred when, as a boy, he helped drive cattle across the northern end of the desert. When a young man, he found a job driving one of the legendary twenty-mule teams that hauled borax out of the desert. But now he had plans for a grand swindle. He started claiming he had discovered a lost gold mine in Death Valley, and as evidence he displayed chunks of the precious metal. He didn't reveal they were actually pieces of the ore his wife received as a gift in Colorado. That might have spoiled the story.

The Kentuckian's natural talents for fast talking and ingratiating himself to others blossomed like a desert flower. In 1902 Scotty received financial backing for his fictitious mine from a New York banker named Julian Gerard, who expected to receive 50 percent of the findings. The miner sent frequent letters asking Gerard for more money, assuring that he was working hard in the mine's secret location and great riches were just around the corner, yet somehow was never able to display the fruits of his labors. About $20,000 later, Gerard got wise and quit financing the mine.

The persuasive Scotty then managed in 1904 to win the support of deeply religious Chicago multi-millionaire Albert M. Johnson, president of the National Life Insurance Company of America, who gave the prospector a grubstake of $20,000. This was to begin a lifelong friendship that was both touching and inexplicable. Johnson realized quite soon that Scotty was taking him for a ride. The strange thing is, he didn't seem to mind. He was only too happy to pay for the miner's whims and fancies, knowing well Scotty would never be able to pay him back. Johnson simply enjoyed basking in Scotty's ebullient personality.

In the meanwhile, Scotty developed a reputation for being a wild spender. He would often travel to Los Angeles, where he threw money around with tremendous ostentation, or at least pretended to. He would tip bellboys with halves of $50 bills, and then surreptitiously buy back the halves for $20 each. Scotty was not rich, but he was eager to put up the appearance of having untold wealth. The money he spent was "borrowed" from first Gerard and then Johnson, not earned from laboring in a mine.

Many were convinced by the miner's deceptions and word got around that Scotty knew the location of a secret gold mine. Those who believed his stories trailed him through the desert, hoping to find its location. This included a number of scouts and Indians, some hired and some acting on their own volition. None of them ever came away with anything more than severe sunburn, but Scotty would spin pretty tales of having been ambushed and shot three times, losing a Shoshone Indian companion to murderous blackguards, and having to watch his back constantly. He also told of having been snakebit twice and bitten on the ear by a rabid skunk, which at least sounds plausible. In addition, the prospector pretended to have been robbed of $12,000 worth of gold dust, possibly as an excuse for lacking the riches one would expect of a man who had access to a private mine.

Scotty may have stretched the truth where his gold mine scam was concerned, but he became a celebrity by legitimate means in July 1905 when he set a speed record for railway travel. He rented the Santa Fe Railroad's Coyote Special for $5,500 with the intention of riding the train from Los Angeles to Chicago in 45 hours or less. The $5,500 deposit was not his own money, of course, though Scotty gave the impression it was earnings from his gold mine. The railroad promised to refund $500 if the locomotive was unable to set the new record. Scotty, the engineer, and a fireman, accompanied by the miner's yellow dog, sped across the rails on a shortened train consisting of the engine, a baggage car, a dining car, and a Pullman sleeping car. The stunt just barely succeeded, as he made the trip in 44 hours and 54 minutes. The record remained unbroken for 29 years.

Once in Chicago, Scotty was treated to a hero's welcome. He told the press his first "pard," banker Julian Gerard, was getting his share of the mine's profits, a blatant falsehood. Despite his promise to "show Chicagoans how to throw away money," Scotty "did not rid himself of enough wealth to excite interest," according to the *New York Times,* more evidence the prospector did not have unlimited wealth as he wanted everyone to believe.

After reuniting with his wife, Scotty took a trip to New York where he was again feted by the citizens. He was given to making folksy statements to the press, such as "What will they think when Scotty says he don't care much about the Waldorf? They didn't know what dollar tips were until he showed them. I showed 'em, and showed 'em right, and then I gave 'em the laugh..." The *Times,* for one, was not fooled. An editorial read, "The Death Valley Live One's naiveté is all too obviously a somewhat laborious pose, assumed for reasons not yet revealed.... His rough and uncomfortable clothes are almost surely the costuming of a part, and for his long-heralded determination to separate himself from as much of his money as fast and as soon as he can, his acts provide no large amount of confirmation."

Concerning the alleged millionaire's niggardly spending habits, the *Times* further noted that he gave generous tips only rarely, and that "at his present pace a few thousand dollars will keep him going for some time to come." Then the newspaper hit an editorial bullseye. "To the cynical and suspicious the indications are that the object of Mr. Scott's visit is to get wealth rather than to get rid of it." The *Times* speculated that he was trying to sell wildcat stock in his fabled mine, though in reality a New York mining outfit secretly paid for Scotty's trip on the locomotive in return for his advertising their company, as he admitted before a grand jury in 1912.

Bizarre events involving Scotty continued to proliferate. In late August 1905, a wanderer in the desert named W.T. Mills claimed to have accidentally stumbled across the location of Scotty's secret gold mine. Newspapers trumpeted this exciting information, and hundreds of prospectors rushed to the site. However, Mills did not bring back any gold to support his statement, as one might expect, and it was speculated that he found a claim belonging to someone else and merely assumed it was Scotty's. As the papers were suspiciously silent concerning the outcome, we can only conclude that Mills was mistaken or a hoaxer. On October 30 of the same year, the famous prospector was injured in a car crash. It was reported that he broke his neck and was near death, and yet he was known to have been back in his camp on December 1, barely a month later, so the extent of his injuries must have been overstated. On December 7, Scotty's mule ambled into the miner's camp, without rider but sporting a bloody blanket and saddle. In addition, the saddle had a bullet hole in it. Scotty was missing a number of days, and everyone thought the worst— plenty more newspaper headlines in scarehead type— but on Christmas Day, a friend of Scotty's in Los Angeles received a letter from the prospector claiming he had been shot in an ambush but not seriously wounded. There appears to be no evidence except his own word for it that Scotty was actually shot, so one can be forgiven for concluding the disappearance was a staged incident. Like many less-than-talented modern celebrities, after he got a taste of the limelight Scotty learned to do outrageous things every so often to make sure his name stayed in the headlines.

Even after several years of being bilked, the amiable Johnson continued to support his friend Scotty. Many have speculated that the millionaire was generous with Scotty out of gratitude. When the miner

first asked for a prospecting grubstake in 1904, Johnson was in bad health due to an injury received in a train wreck. Scotty's descriptions of Death Valley so intrigued Johnson that he took a yearly vacation to the desert, partly to regain his health and partly to visit Scotty. The dry air and desert climate helped him recover his strength. Eventually Albert Johnson and his wife Bessie moved to Death Valley, where he continued to be entertained by the miner's showman-like personality and schemes.

The grandest scheme of all was hatched in 1922. Death Valley Scotty wanted to build a mansion in the middle of the desert. It is one thing for an eccentric to have an obsessive vision, but if an eccentric can convince someone else to pay for his obsession— now *that* is salesmanship. With the indulgent Johnson footing the bills, construction began on a Spanish-Moorish style stucco house complete with red tiled roof and nine spires, one of which is a clock tower 56 feet high. The mansion has 33,000 square feet of space, which includes a cavernous reception lounge, numerous bathrooms with tiled floors and a garage. The construction was accomplished by laborers from Los Angeles and local Shoshone and Paiute Indians. Craftsmen were imported from Austria to carve the house's woodwork, and much of the furniture is from Spain. The yard was landscaped with trees not native to the area, including plum and fig, and featured a guest house with a veranda. In order to fuel the mansion's 18 fireplaces, Johnson purchased 120,000 railroad ties when the Tonopah and Tidewater Railroad went out of business, and had the wood stacked up outside.

Many of the mansion's features are clever. Two weathervanes feature the metal likeness of Scotty in the act of rounding up burros. There is a second-floor balcony providing a fine view of the grounds. The living room contains a fountain and a fish pool. One room was built specifically to house a massive pipe organ intended for theaters. The builders even provided for electricity, supplied by the moving waters of the Grapevine Springs.

Because of the remote location of the site, nearly all building materials had to be hauled in from outside the desert over a period of several years at an estimated cost of between $2 and $3 million. Work came to a screeching halt in 1931 when a survey team found the house inadvertently had been built on government land.

Death Valley was declared a national monument in 1933, and the government agreed to allow Johnson to purchase the land on which Scotty's Castle rested for only $1.25 per acre. Johnson did so, but his insurance business was damaged by the Great Depression, and as a result the mansion remains unfinished to this day. Oddly, Scotty himself lived in the castle only sporadically, often dwelling in a redwood shack five miles from the mansion.

In order to make some money from their (that is to say, Johnson's) investment, Scotty and the insurance executive opened the completed portion of their desert castle as a tourist attraction. It was an immediate success as one of the few marks of civilization in a wilderness of torturous heat, and remains a popular site today. The old prospector finally found his gold mine, but not in the way he expected.

In February 1930, Scotty announced he was broke due to the stock market crash. In a rare moment of absolute truthfulness, he admitted to the press there was no secret mine and never had been, and also confessed he had been living off Johnson's largesse for years. Soon, however, he was again pretending to be a self-made millionaire.

Scotty received unwanted publicity in January 1937, when he was sued for separate maintenance by the long-abandoned Mrs. Scott, late of Reno, Nv., and then Long Beach, Ca. Since her errant husband's alleged wealth had been estimated at $1 million, 60-year-old Mrs. Scott wanted $1,000 a month for living expenses and medical care, plus $25,000 for legal expenses and a division of property. He had often promised he would come back to her and settle down when he raised his stake. (This was the same man who boasted publicly about his profligate spending. He was seemingly untroubled by the contradiction.) But, said Mrs. Scott, "When I read of his plans to build that fantastic castle in the desert I knew that gold and notoriety and his business deals had finally wiped me out of his heart."

The true state of Scotty's dubious finances became one of the major mysteries for the court to unravel, and in the process Albert Johnson was called to the stand on January 14. Under oath, he admitted "Scotty hasn't got a dime. I've been paying his bills for years. He repaid me in laughs, and I like him." Johnson further revealed the miner did not even own the title to the car he drove, and that over the past 30 years he had given Scotty $1.5 million. Mrs. Scott left the courthouse no wealthier than when she arrived. Scarcely a week later Scotty offered to pay for some drinks in a Tucson, Az., bar with a $10,000 bill.

In March 1940, after satisfying the Internal Revenue Service that he had no income for 30 years and had been sponging off his friend Johnson all that time, Scotty told the government that he suddenly remembered burying $100,000 worth of gold certificates in the Death Valley mountains around 1909, but cloudbursts had caused it to be lost. He asked the IRS if the money would still be honored as legal tender if he ever found it. This was another tall tale, it seems. Neither Scott nor anyone else ever found a trace of the putative lost treasure.

Scotty found himself in more trouble in August 1940. His first business partner, Julian Gerard, sued over the grubstake he had given the miner nearly 40 years previously. When the case came to trial in Los

Angeles in March 1941, Scotty again told the truth about his mine before Judge Benjamin Harrison, who demanded to know:

"Have you a mine now?'

"No, sir."

"Did you ever have a mine?"

"No, except in the Knickerbocker claims in the mountains."

"Did you ever take any gold out of the ground and sell it?"

"I never sold any gold."

"How much money have you taken from mining ventures over the years?"

"None, and I have no secret mine."

The next day in court, Judge Harrison called Scotty a "cheat" who defrauded Gerard with his letters promising imminent wealth. On June 11, the judge ruled that Gerard was entitled to 22-and-a-half percent interest in Scotty's mining claims, "if any exist." And of course, since they did not exist, that meant Gerard won nearly 25 percent of nothing. Perhaps he felt it was a moral victory. Judge Harrison also ruled that Gerard was not entitled to any part of Scotty's Castle since the original contract concerned only mining. (Also, the castle was actually owned by Johnson.) The judge could not resist using an extended mining analogy when summing up the case. He said, "Scott first discovered a prospect in the person of Gerard, but paydirt soon pinched out. But when he discovered Johnson he uncovered a large body of paying ore that is still producing excellent mint returns. The only difference between Gerard and Johnson is that Johnson apparently enjoys watching his protege bask in the glitter of his gold."

After this final legal predicament, life for Scotty became mellow. Since his adventure with the speeding train in 1905, Death Valley Scotty had been gradually transformed into a living legend, as famous as fellow nickname-bearing westerners such as Wild Bill Hickock, Calamity Jane, or Billy the Kid. For years, Scotty himself was one of the biggest tourist attractions in the area. He would stay at the castle which bore his name and spin yarns for visitors lucky enough to catch a glimpse of him. Dane Coolidge wrote in 1937: "The biggest man in Death Valley is Scotty. Whether he has a mine or not, whether he ever had a mine or not, he overshadows the rest of the prospectors the way his castle does a tenthouse. No matter if the castle isn't his, or if he gets all his money from Johnson, he is just naturally *big* and he has picked the right place to be big in.... The first question people ask when you come back from Death Valley is: 'Did you see Scotty?' If you did, your vacation was a success. If not you are just another tourist."

Eventually the Johnsons moved to Hollywood, giving their old friend run of the mansion. Albert, benefactor and willing dupe, died in 1948. Death Valley Scotty, the greatest showman and self-promoter the West had seen since Buffalo Bill, followed suit on January 5, 1954, due to a gastro-intestinal hemorrhage. He is buried on a hill overlooking his beloved "shack," as he liked to call the castle. The region has been explored countless times by government surveyors and freelance parties; no trace of Scotty's great lost gold mine has ever been found, and doubtless never will be. The prospector was, as biographer Hank Johnston wittily dubbed him, "The Fastest Con in the West."

Speedy Atkins

Corpse

Paducah, May 30, 1928. A 37-year-old mortician named A.Z. Hamock has received word that the body of a man in his fifties has been pulled from the Ohio River at the foot of Campbell Street. The dead man was found by W.P. Howe, who while out fishing saw the corpse entangled in the beams of the Illinois Central railway trestle. Before long, the corpse is brought to the funeral home for embalming. Although the body has been partially submerged for three days, Hamock recognizes the man. He is Charles Henry Atkins of 1031 Kentucky Avenue, an indigent black man who was a worker at the Dixon Tobacco Company. Atkins is known to the town as "Speedy" because he is— was— a fast worker. Coroner R.L. Nelson informs Hamock that on the last day of his life, around May 28, Atkins had gone fishing near Owens Island. He made the mistake of bringing along a cheering jar of home-brewed liquor. After drinking a little too much, Atkins fell first asleep and then into the river.

Upon inquiry, Hamock finds that Speedy has no next-of-kin whatsoever to claim his body or pay for a burial. It looks like Atkins must be buried in the local potter's field at city expense. But then Hamock has an idea. For years he has been fascinated by the accounts of the mummification performed by ancient Egyptian embalmers. Also for years, he has been creating his own super-strength embalming fluid.

Why not try it out on the unclaimed body of Speedy Atkins and see how well it works?

Over 70 years later, one must say that Hamock's experiment was a resounding success. Speedy's body was so well preserved that he was not buried until 1994, nearly 70 years after his death. In the interim, he reached a level of celebrity that many living people would envy.

After Hamock embalmed Speedy using his secret formula, he kept the body in a back room so he could check it periodically. Within a few months, the corpse had more or less petrified. Once it became apparent that Speedy's body was simply not going to decompose,

Offbeat Kentuckians

Hamock dressed him up in some natty clothes and placed him in a closet at the funeral home. As years passed, Speedy took on a shrunken, leathery appearance, his face fixed in an expression approximating a grin. In fact, he bore a startling resemblance to an unwrapped Egyptian mummy. A.Z. Hamock's chemicals did their work very well. The only maintenance required was a thorough washing three times a year to stave off the effects of mold.

Naturally, word got around concerning Speedy, and soon Hamock's received a steady stream of curious visitors who wanted to see the sprucely dressed cadaver for themselves. Sometimes tourists arrived by the busload. No one left disappointed. Soon articles about Speedy Atkins were appearing in newspapers and national magazines. Hamock never charged admission to see the body. Museums and carnivals often expressed interest in buying Speedy's remains, but Hamock always turned them down. A Paducah resident named Gladman Humbles who knew the funeral director in the 1940s recalled that Hamock always told would-be purchasers that slavery was over, and therefore he was not going into the business of selling humans.

Hamock died in 1949, refusing to the last to divulge the secret of his embalming formula. His widow Velma took over the family business of running the funeral home. (Hamock's is, incidentally, the oldest continuously operating black-owned business in Paducah.) She kept up her late husband's tradition of showing Speedy to his fans, many of whom traveled hundreds of miles for that purpose. Like her husband, she did not charge money to see Speedy.

The body had some interesting adventures over the years. The 1937 Paducah flood carried him away, but he was eventually found unscathed, mute testimony to the power of Hamock's embalming fluid. Mrs. Hamock appeared on national TV with Speedy three times: on ABC's "That's Incredible" in 1980, on CNN in 1989 and on the syndicated "A Current Affair" in 1991.

In August 1994, the 100th anniversary of the founding of Hamock's Funeral Home, Velma Hamock made a momentous decision: it was finally time to give Speedy a proper burial. As she explained to a reporter, "He is a dead person, and there is no need to keep on keeping on." On August 5, Speedy Atkins received a memorial service at the

Washington Street Baptist Church, the Rev. Raynarldo Henderson presiding. The estimated 200 persons who attended the visitation beheld Speedy all dressed up in a tuxedo and lying in state within an elegant casket. The Rev. H. Joseph Franklin eulogized. He said Speedy "came to Paducah a pauper, poor, homeless, a nobody. Today, he's going to be laid to rest at last, as a celebrity."

The affection the community had for the long dead Speedy Atkins was touching. Local businesses donated the money to purchase his plot, funeral and casket. A letter was sent to Hamock's from a Baltimore woman named Ella L. Simmons, who knew Speedy when she was only five years old and he boarded at her grandparents' house. According to Simmons, Atkins was a kind man who gave his spare pennies to her and a sister. She remembered him as a man who loved children.

After the services, Atkins was buried in Paducah's Maplelawn Cemetery. Mrs. Hamock told the press, "I never saw a dead man bring so much happiness to people."

And that's how Speedy Atkins, who had no family to love or care for him, became a man loved and cared for by thousands.

Tod Browning

Director

The 1931 motion picture *Dracula* retains its status as one of the most famous movies ever made. It ushered in the golden age of horror films, made an international sensation of its star Bela Lugosi, and has been remade several times. Yet how many viewers are aware that the man who directed this and many other classic horror films was a Kentuckian?

His real name was Charles Albert Browning, but he will be known to film buffs forever by his adopted name, Tod Browning. He was born in Louisville on July 12, 1880 (some sources claim 1881). Browning was always a very private and mysterious figure. In one of his few interviews he commented that "only stars should be interviewed because they have the glamour that directors lack," but the few details that are known about his childhood sound like a plot from a very strange movie. While no one can be certain, it appears young Browning did not get along well with his family. After he became a wealthy and famous director, he spurned them almost entirely, returning to Louisville to visit only a couple of times and flatly refusing to attend family members' funerals. (His uncle Pete Browning, incidentally, was an outstanding early baseball player whose batting average compares favorably to Babe Ruth's. He was nicknamed "The Louisville Slugger," and the famous bat of the same name was originally developed for his use.)

One childhood incident that must surely have left its mark on the young boy's psyche was the fearsome Louisville tornado of March 27, 1890, which killed nearly 100 people and struck only a few blocks from the Browning residence.

After working for a saddler, Browning ran away from home in late 1899 or early 1900 to join a circus. He found employment for several years as a clown, dancer, barker, contortionist, acrobat and ringmaster. One of his carnival acts required that he be "hypnotized" and buried alive on a regular basis.

To further his marketability in the entertainment industry, Browning later joined the Whirl of Mirth vaudeville troupe. His experiences in the circus and in vaudeville would later influence the deeply personal vision he put on film. There were other influences developing in this stage of his life as well, for Browning was becoming addicted to alcohol, and he endured the hardships faced by the average impoverished actor on the road. In later years, Browning would relate an incident that made an indelible impression: once while temporarily boarding in an actors' hotel, he entered the bathroom only to discover an insane woman in the act of fatally cutting her two children's throats.

By the time Browning entered vaudeville, that form of live entertainment was dying due to the burgeoning motion picture industry. Like many other performers, Browning realized the wisest course of action would be to try acting in films rather than on the stage. In 1913, Browning went to the Biograph Studio in New York and began doing bit roles as a slapstick comedian under the supervision of D.W. Griffith, a fellow Kentuckian who was using technical and storytelling innovations to transform the motion picture from a lowbrow amusement into a genuine art form.

The director liked Browning, and when he moved his base of operations to Hollywood, Ca., in October 1913, Browning came along. Griffith encouraged the young man to write scripts as well as act. He also let Browning work as an assistant director on some pictures, placing him among other Griffith acolytes who went on to greater glory, including Erich von Stroheim, Allan Dwan and Victor Fleming. Browning was one of the assistant directors working on Griffith's epic

Intolerance (1916). In that film's modern sequence, he can be seen playing the owner of a racing car who loans his vehicle to friends of a wrongly condemned man who must rush to stop his execution.

In reality, a speeding car had been an instrument of destruction rather than salvation in Browning's life. On the night of June 16, 1915, the director careened through the streets of Los Angeles in his car. He was drunk and the night was foggy. Browning plowed head-on into a truck loaded with iron rails. His passenger was Elmer Booth, a Griffith actor who had been the star of the very first gangster film, *The Musketeers of Pig Alley* (1912). Booth was killed instantly; Hollywood gossip had it that his head was indented like a waffle by the impact when he crashed into the iron poles. Browning suffered from severe lower-body injuries, including three fractures in one leg. It took him nearly a year to fully recover.

Exactly how Browning was affected by the fact that he accidentally killed his friend, we will never know. An intensely secretive man, he seems to have never told anyone his thoughts on the subject. However, his biographers David Skal and Elias Savada note that while Browning directed mostly comedies and light romances before the wreck, his favorite subject matter afterward tended to involve death and grim retribution for criminal acts.

In 1917 Browning directed his first feature-length film, *Jim Bludso*. Gradually he began directing films for Universal, and for that studio he made *The Wicked Darling*. The movie starred Lon Chaney, famed as "The Man Of A Thousand Faces," an excellent pantomimist who was willing to undergo torturous physical transformations via makeup in order to portray frightening and/or sympathetic characters onscreen. The film was a hit.

It was apparent Browning had a feel for dark, atmospheric melodramas and horror films, so he and Chaney were teamed up repeatedly throughout their careers. Their ten silent productions together included *The Wicked Darling* (1919), *Outside The Law* (1921), *The Unholy Three* (1925), *The Blackbird* (1926), *The Road to Mandalay* (1926), *The Unknown* (1927), *London After Midnight* (1927), *West of Zanzibar* (1928), *The Big City* (1928), and *Where East Is East* (1929). The first two films were made by Universal Studios, and the remaining eight were M-G-M productions. Nearly all of the films had scripts that were either written by Browning or were based on one of his original ideas.

Throughout his career the director also helmed a number of lightweight comedies and action pictures in addition to the films with darker subject matter, but some of the movies he made with Chaney bear closer examination because they provide hints as to the macabre workings of the mind of Browning. *The Unholy Three* has a plot that reflects the director's early experiences with carnival life: three circus performers are also professional criminals. Chaney plays a ventriloquist who disguises himself in the film as an old woman, and a real-life little person named Harry Earles portrays a midget who pretends to be the ventriloquist's dummy and doubles as a baby in order to steal jewels. The third criminal of the title is the strongman.

The Unknown, while containing similar motifs, is even stranger and has a story line that would make the fortune of a Freudian analyst. It gives weight to critic Stuart Rosenthal's remark that "Browning is so aggressive and unrelenting in his pursuit of certain themes that he

appears to be neurotically fixated on them." In the film, Chaney is Alonzo, a criminal desperate to hide from the police. He is able-bodied except for one deformity: he has a double thumb. The fugitive joins a circus and masquerades as an armless sideshow attraction who performs a knife-tossing act with his feet. The target of his knives during the act is Nanon (Joan Crawford), the circus owner's daughter. As part of the show, Alonzo shoots a rifle with such accuracy that each bullet cuts off a piece of Nanon's revealing costume. Complications arise when Alonzo falls in love with Nanon, who has a morbid fear of being touched by men. He is under the delusion that she will love him as long as she believes he is truly armless. Eventually, after strangling Nanon's abusive father, Alonzo blackmails a surgeon into amputating his arms for real, only to find Nanon has since overcome her fear of being touched with help from the circus strongman.

London After Midnight may have been something of a master-piece for both Browning and Chaney. In this film, the actor plays a detective posing as a vampire; the makeup required was painful even by Chaney's notorious standards. A couple of thin wires were used to make his eyes bulge abnormally, and he wore an agonizing set of false teeth with pointed, ratchet-like fangs that he could stand to wear only for a few minutes at a time.

The movie received rave reviews, and a British judge mentioned the film specifically when commenting on a real-life murder case. In October 1928, a lunatic named Robert Williams slashed the throat of an Irish housemaid, Julia Mangan, in Hyde Park. Williams claimed he killed her while in an epileptic fit, during which he had been terrified by a vision of Lon Chaney. The judge, Justice Humphries, addressed the jury: "If Williams saw the film *London After Midnight*, in which Chaney takes the part of a detective who pretends to be a terrifying ghost, you may not think it remarkable or indicating insanity that he should in a moment of emotional excitement remember the horrifying aspect of the actor in a part in which he is being purposely terrible." (The jury sentenced Williams to death, but he was reprieved three weeks later.) Modern viewers are unable to judge the movie's frightfulness for themselves, as *London After Midnight* is one of Browning's missing films.

It is evident that despite his quiet and private nature, Browning had a grotesque imagination without peer in the Hollywood of the 1920s. In an era before the advent of the film *auteur*, most directors were expected to turn out wholesome, agreeable films as though on an assembly line, preferably on time and under budget. In the 20s only a few acclaimed directors were given free rein to make films according to their own personal vision. (This included such geniuses of drama as Griffith, Cecil B. DeMille, and Erich von Stroheim, and also the comedians Charlie Chaplin, Harold Lloyd, and Buster Keaton.) Though he never became a household name, Browning was one of the lucky few who had a level of freedom most directors never knew. He could create films based on his own story ideas and, as Diane MacIntyre wrote, "Browning liked to integrate ideas that tended to push the envelope of depravity and masochism. Revenge, self-sacrifice, frigidity, amputation, freaks, murder, dwarfs, sideshows and the like were part of the Browning vocabulary of creativity." She might have added the recurring themes of deception, disguise, deformity, petty crime and death. Of the 10 films Browning made with Chaney, half feature a main character who is crippled or scarred in some way *(Road to Mandalay, The Unknown, The Blackbird, West of Zanzibar,* and *Where East is East.)* In at least seven of the films, the lead character is also a criminal. Because of his love for offbeat subject material and his insistence on atmospheric art direction, Browning might be considered the forerunner of such modern directors as David Lynch and Tim Burton.

Not everyone, of course, was taken with Browning's taste for morbid and bizarre film plots. *The Unknown* garnered some typical backhanded reviews. *Variety* complained: "Every time Browning thinks of Chaney he probably looks around for a typewriter and says 'Let's get gruesome.'" *Harrison's Reports* deemed it "unpleasant." And the *New York Times*'s critic noted that it was "anything but a pleasant story. It is gruesome and at times shocking, and the principal character deteriorates from a more or less sympathetic individual to an arch-fiend." However, Browning earned enough good reviews and enough fans who appreciated his style to earn the nickname "The Edgar Allan Poe of cinema."

Though Browning's star was rising, there were clouds on the horizon. He and Chaney got along well as collaborators, but it was also true that Chaney's two greatest successes were made without Browning: *The Hunchback of Notre Dame* (1923) and *The Phantom of the Opera* (1925). This led some spectators to conclude Chaney was the real genius of the pair. It is likely Browning's reputation as a hard drinker kept him from getting the assignment to direct *Hunchback.*

But a greater problem arose when the director became too bold for Hollywood's comfort. In the golden era of filmmaking, movie plots were tailored for specific stars in regards to the expectations of their fans. Stories full of death, mutilation and criminals in disguise worked fine in a Chaney picture, because his fans expected nothing less. However, in 1927 Browning was given the chance to direct a film starring John Gilbert, who at the time was M-G-M's top male box office attraction. Browning's idea of a suitable plot was *The Show,* which cast the matinee idol in an unsympathetic role as a circus con artist. Not only that, the film insisted on presenting sideshow freaks as major characters. The critics, Gilbert's fans and Gilbert himself expressed displeasure with the film. Unhappy M-G-M executives had their first hint that Browning's dark vision, if misapplied, could be box office poison.

In 1930 Chaney made his first (and only) talking film, a remake of *The Unholy Three.* The movie again featured Harry Earles as the criminally inclined midget, but Browning did not direct. The film was a success, largely because it proved Chaney was as versatile with his voice as he was with his physical appearance. Impressed by both the financial triumph of *The Unholy Three* and the public's burgeoning interest in talking horror movies, Universal Studios asked the master of the macabre, Browning, to make a film based on the theatrical adaptation of Bram Stoker's novel *Dracula.*

Browning wanted Chaney to portray the vampire, but the actor died unexpectedly of a throat hemorrhage on August 6, 1930. The actor who got the role, of course, was Bela Lugosi. Modern audiences find the film difficult to sit through, and most critics agree the direction is too stagy, probably because Browning chose to adhere closely to the play's version of the story. (*Dracula* was a rare exercise for Browning because he was making a horror film that was not based on one of his own original stories.) Only the film's first reel, which takes place in the vampire's Transylvanian castle, displays the director's talent for creating an eerie,

169

disturbing atmosphere. (To be fair, some film historians claim much of the credit should rightfully go to the movie's cameraman, Karl Freund.) When Universal's brass saw the finished film, they were afraid the public would be disgusted by Browning's vampire epic, and chose to downplay the fact that it was a horror film. It was advertised simply as "The story of the strangest passion the world has ever known." Nevertheless, audiences in 1931 had never seen anything like *Dracula,* and the film was a stunning success; it became Universal's top grossing film of the year. It looked as though Browning had again hit his stride as a surefire moneymaker, and the director was restored to M-G-M's good graces—at least temporarily. M-G-M gave him *carte blanche* for his next project, which would prove a major mistake for both Browning and the studio.

Having not learned a lesson from the debacle over his film *The Show,* which featured supporting actors merely playing circus freaks, Browning decided to make a melodrama that was specifically about circus freaks. And he was no longer content to settle for actors with competent makeup jobs. This film would star authentic sideshow attractions, the kind he came to know so well during his own youthful days with the circus. When Louis B. Mayer, head of M-G-M, got wind of Browning's pet project, he immediately objected that such a film would be much too terrifying for audiences. It was not the sort of film he wanted associated with his studio, famous for its glamorous fare. Surely, he must have argued, most people would rather look at Greta Garbo than a bearded lady or a legless wonder. However, production head Irving Thalberg convinced Mayer to let the director have his way. It was "one of the few times his famous instinct let him down," as film writer John Brosnan notes.

Browning's insistence on hiring real circus performers for *Freaks* meant the film has one of the strangest casts ever assembled. The movie features a number of midgets, including the aforementioned Earles; Violet and Daisy Hilton, the Siamese twins; Prince Randian, an armless and legless performer; Pete Robinson, a living skeleton; Johnny Eck, a boy with half a torso; Olga Roderick, a bearded lady; the Turtle Girl; Josephine-Joseph, the half-woman, half-man; Koo Koo the Bird Girl; and a variety of assorted pinheads. During the film's production, the cast was banned from the M-G-M studio commissary. This decision to ban freaks was destined to seem bitterly ironic several months later after the film's release.

The plot of *Freaks* was based on a story called "Spurs" by Tod Robbins and contained many elements dear to Browning's heart: a midget named Hans has fallen in love with the beautiful trapeze artist, Cleopatra, who marries him for his money and then humiliates him by flaunting her attraction to Hercules the circus strongman. The "normal" lovers attempt to poison Hans in order to get his inheritance money, but the other freaks in the sideshow catch wind of the plot and take action. During a nighttime thunderstorm, the gun-and-knife-wielding freaks advance on the terrified pair and extract a ghastly revenge. The once physically perfect Cleopatra is transformed into a freak herself, the legless, clucking "Chicken Woman." The ultimate fate of Hercules is not revealed, but presumably he was murdered. According to John Brosnan, a scene edited from the original ending implied the strongman was turned by the freaks into a singing castrato.

Freaks is now considered one of the greatest of all cult films and is often seen in revival houses, on late-night TV, and on video, but its release in 1932 was an unmitigated disaster. The reasons were manifold. Depression-era audiences could accept make-believe horror involving such creatures as vampires, mummies and Frankenstein's monster, but the vision of real deformity onscreen was simply overwhelming for most viewers. Indeed, to this very day many moviegoers simply cannot handle the matter-of-fact treatment of unpleasant reality presented in *Freaks*. Many have argued that Browning made the same fundamental mistake he made years before in *The Unknown*. He turns his sympathetic characters into villains at the end of the story. The freaks are fascinating people and are presented in a sympathetic and humane light for most of the movie. The point is made repeatedly that they are much kinder and more loyal than the "normal" persons who exploit and make fun of them. But the finale which features them crawling and hopping through the mud, weapons in hand, is truly the stuff of nightmares.

Also, we cannot overlook the disturbing effect of the film's dialogue, which critic Danny Peary noted is laced with as many sexual innuendoes and double entendres as the censors would permit. The dialogue would be surprising in any film from the 1930s, but in the context of the sideshow, it must have —pardon the pun— freaked out many viewers.

It did not take long after the film's release for M-G-M to realize the magnitude of the repulsion *Freaks* inspired. At the film's preview in San Diego, several patrons walked out, and a woman ran screaming from the theater. Another woman attempted to sue M-G-M, claiming the film caused her to have a miscarriage. Critics, exhibitors and audiences were shocked, horrified and scandalized; adjectives such as "disgusting," "nauseating," and "tasteless" appeared in reviews too frequently for the studio's comfort. *Freaks* did good business in some cities, but in other towns the film was banned. (Great Britain took matters to an extreme and prohibited the film for over 30 years.) Desperate for business, the studio's publicity department tried to sell the revenge tale as a romance. The advertisements read: "Can a full-grown woman truly love a midget? Here's the strangest romance in the world— the love story of a giant, a siren, and a midget!" Although the film had cost only $316,000 to produce, it was one of the biggest financial failures in M-G-M's history. After a few weeks, the embarrassed studio caved in to pressure from protesters and withdrew the film from circulation. In some prints of the film seen today, according to Diane MacIntyre, "the M-G-M logo at the beginning has been noticeably camouflaged to disguise the offended studio's identity." At least Irving Thalberg got his wish fulfilled when he told Browning, "Give me something that will out-horror *Frankenstein*."

It would be no exaggeration to say the *Freaks* disaster nearly derailed Browning's career. In retaliation, M-G-M's next assignment for the director under contract was *Fast Workers*, a 1933 romantic comedy starring John Gilbert of Browning's earlier failure *The Show*, and who by then was also on Louis B. Mayer's personal hit list. The plot dealt with high-rise construction workers, clearly not the director's choice of material. The film was a resounding commercial failure.

The "Edgar Allan Poe of the cinema" made only three more films for M-G-M, all of which contain traces of the authentic Browning touch: *Mark of the Vampire* (1935), a remake of *London After Midnight* starring Bela Lugosi; *The Devil-Doll* (1936), co-written by another director who fell from grace with M-G-M, Erich von Stroheim; and

Miracles For Sale (1939). After the last, he retired from the film industry and lived off the fortune he amassed from his Hollywood years. In the words of his biographers Skal and Savada, "In a town that has traditionally worshipped fame, self-aggrandizement, and the glare of publicity, Browning's reclusive career and its dissolution amounted to one of Hollywood's most mysterious vanishing acts."

Browning became ever more publicity-shy in his Santa Monica mansion until he died while recovering from an operation for cancer at age eighty-two on October 6, 1962. Predictably, his obituaries stressed his direction of *Dracula* while largely overlooking the other films in his body of work. A month before Browning died *Freaks*, the film that led to his downfall, was honored at the Venice Film Festival.

Since his death, Browning's reputation has steadily grown. He has his own cult following, which seems only appropriate. In 1995, Skal and Savada published *Dark Carnival*, the most definitive and only full-length biography of Browning, no easy feat considering his reluctance to discuss either himself or his films.

It can be said Browning was one of the true originals to emerge from the golden age of film. His unique vision was tolerated as long as it made money for the studio, but perhaps he should be remembered for helping expand the range of subject matter considered permissible for the movies. Somehow an offhand statement made by Browning in 1929 during one of his rare interviews seems emblematic of his Hollywood career: "It would appear that treading on tradition is the only thing in motion pictures that advances it."

George Barrett

Career Criminal

He "looked more like a Bible salesman than a killer." That's how an Indianapolis reporter described George W. Barrett, a felon from the 1930s who is strangely overlooked today. Had he been a bank robber, a crime that resulted in enormous amounts of attention from the media, Barrett might now have a place alongside John Dillinger, Pretty Boy Floyd and Bonnie and Clyde in the pantheon of Depression-era criminals. Barrett's obscurity is all the more inexplicable when one considers that he was the first murderer in American history to be executed for the specific crime of killing an FBI agent.

Contemporary newspaper accounts provide contradictory information about the events in Barrett's life. Even his age is often given incorrectly. However, census records confirm that he entered the world on February 27, 1887, in Clay County, the son of William G. and Nancy ("Nannie") Barrett. He was the second of seven children. The family moved to Jackson County when Barrett was still a young boy.

Barrett received only a sixth grade education and got married around 1904 when he was 17 years old. The marriage lasted four months, after which he abandoned his wife for another woman. He encountered his first serious trouble with the law in 1913, when he was moonshining even before Prohibition became the law of the land. He

Offbeat Kentuckians

George Barrett at the
time of his trial for
murdering an
FBI agent.
From the *American
Magazine*, April
1937.

was caught in Hardinsburg, but arresting him was no easy matter. Before police finally managed to slip the handcuffs on Barrett, he engaged in a shootout that cost him an eye. Allegedly one of Barrett's pursuers was a cousin.

Just after Barrett received his ghastly injury, his sister Sylvania came to his aid. She was later arrested on a charge of interfering with law enforcement officers and sentenced to serve nearly a year in the Breckinridge County jail. (Another account claims Barrett lost his eye in a much later fight, and that a brother-in-law named Marion Brewer was the one who did the shooting.) Barrett served 30 days in jail and paid a $100 fine. He was arrested for the same offense in the town of Clifton Mills on April 15, 1913.

The missing eye would not be his last serious injury. By the end of his life, Barrett's body would bear the traces of 20 bullet wounds received in various fights.

After a stint in the army, around 1917 Barrett moved to

Cincinnati, Ohio, and lived with a brother in the suburb of Hamilton. Barrett found work as a streetcar conductor. Despite the job's lowly salary, he somehow managed to acquire and flaunt so many diamonds that Hamilton police nicknamed him "The Diamond King." Barrett came up with a multitude of nefarious methods for subsidizing his taste for jewelry. For example, he fenced stolen goods at cut-rate prices on his streetcar. He started out small by selling rings and watches, but later his ambition led him to sell stolen diamonds. He cultivated a habit of purchasing diamond rings from jewelry stores, then removing the diamonds and replacing them with fakes. Barrett would return a ring, get his money refunded, and later sell the pilfered gems. Allegedly, he also sold stolen firearms to criminals and smuggled Mexican valuables.

Barrett was known to return occasionally to his first love, bootlegging whisky. In 1929 he was caught by Prohibition agents and was wounded while attempting to escape. He paid a $100 fine and spent a year in prison.

These activities kept Barrett in pocket money and ostentatiously displayed jewelry through the 1920s. He usually walked around with a huge roll of money, sometimes up to $1,000, and made sure everyone knew he had it. Barrett had in the interim married for a second time, but he abandoned his second wife as well. A third woman, a Cincinnatian, bore him a son named Jack in 1923, but for a change, she deserted Barrett in 1929 and ran off with a local butcher. Some time after this turn of events, Barrett remarried one of his ex-wives, then abandoned her again after only four months. A 1930 newspaper article makes the improbable claim that Barrett was married nine times and had additional children in Illinois, Kentucky and Idaho.

Fencing, bootlegging, stealing diamonds, gun running and smuggling were profitable pastimes for Barrett, but he was not averse to murder when it served his purposes or when his temper got the better of him. In his lifetime he killed at least three people for certain, possibly four. Barrett himself boasted that his tally was five or six. His list of known victims included his own mother.

Though he lived in Ohio most of the time and occasionally took extended trips to Idaho, Barrett traveled to Kentucky often to visit his relatives. They probably wished he hadn't. Barrett had left his son to be reared by his mother, Nannie Barrett. In June or July 1930, Barrett dropped in to see his mother and his son in Jackson County and decided to stay at home for a while. The result was a violent domestic dispute at his family's house in Clover Bottom. For several days, Barrett argued with his mother and sister over some now-forgotten matters. He threatened to kill them, and they were frightened enough to travel to McKee where they attempted to swear out a warrant. Barrett then became peaceable, temporarily.

Around 8:30 in the morning of September 2, in the presence of Barrett, Nannie Barrett spanked her seven-year-old grandson Jack for being rude. Barrett screamed that no one had the right to touch his son and browbeat his mother over her notions of child discipline. Barrett's sister, 34-year-old Mrs. Rachel Maupin, unwisely entered the argument stating, "Ma's been good to the boy, George. Why do you pick on her?"

Upon hearing this, Barrett became infuriated. Picking up a .38 caliber pistol, he fired five shots, hitting his 73-year-old mother in the chest, mouth and abdomen. She fell dead on the kitchen floor. Then Barrett gave his hysterical sister a beating with the butt of the gun, shattering her skull. He also shot her through the left ear. Rachel fled the house despite her injuries and climbed aboard Gilbert Alcorn's passing mail truck, which was headed for the town of McKee. Barrett fired five more shots with a rifle at the departing truck. He hit the vehicle repeatedly, but through sheer luck no shots hit either Alcorn or Rachel.

Barrett's young nephew John was in the house at the time. (One account gives his name as Harding Barrett.) Hearing the commotion, the boy called for Barrett's brothers Lee and Gilbert, who were working in a nearby field. As they approached the house, Barrett coolly told them what he had done and swore he would do the same to them if they "bothered" him. He then changed into some clean clothes, got into his 1930 Chevrolet Sedan, and drove away with his personal arsenal of four pistols and a Winchester rifle. After he left, his shaken brothers called the police. Lee and Gilbert helped search for Barrett and along with county authorities offered a $500 reward for his capture. (The state contributed an additional $200 to the reward.) According to the *Berea Citizen* of September 4, the Barrett brothers requested the police to "shoot to kill and ask questions afterwards."

The wanted posters described Barrett as partially bald with graying hair, 5'9", and weighing 175 pounds. He was a "neat dresser, good talker, pleasant personality, has the appearance of a business man." And of course, the writer did not fail to mention Barrett's glass eye.

While on the lam, Barrett stopped at Clark's general store at Big Hill and spoke with the clerk, James Willie Marcum, as if nothing out of the ordinary had just happened. (Barrett had stopped at the store earlier that morning, before the shootings, to purchase groceries.) The clerk told police that when Barrett left, he was heading in the direction of Berea and Richmond. Later the police received a tip that he had been seen in Paint Lick. That was the last anyone saw of Barrett for several months.

His sister Rachel died of pneumonia at the Berea College Hospital six weeks after the shootings. Barrett turned himself in to the authorities in Jackson County on April 28, 1931. Cynics said he waited until he was sure his sister would be unable to testify against him. Reportedly, he had been hiding in California and Tacoma, Wa.

Barrett was tried twice for the two murders in McKee; the final trial was in January 1932. He claimed he committed the murders in self-defense. Two juries failed to reach a verdict, and Barrett was set free. The prosecutor during the trial happened to be Barrett's own cousin, Commonwealth's Attorney Frank Baker. Probably out of family loyalty, Baker turned in a lackluster performance when prosecuting Barrett. Even the judge was moved to comment that Baker "sounded as though he was defending the accused."

Later, the one-eyed killer was heard to remark that it cost him $1,700 "to bribe two of my relatives so they wouldn't tell the truth on the witness stand."

Although Barrett was acquitted, suspicion fell upon him again when on September 18, 1932, attorney Frank Baker was publicly murdered in a shootout during the "Battle of Manchester," a spectacular event in Clay County's Baker-White family feud. Though Barrett himself took part in the five-hour gunfight in the courthouse square, it was rumored that he had killed his own cousin for unknown reasons. Barrett was arrested and tried twice, but again both juries failed to convict and he walked free.

Offbeat Kentuckians

Barrett's acquittal meant that he was free to continue his one-man crime spree. In 1934 he was arrested in Hazard for selling firearms without a permit. In July 1935 he was fined $50 for possessing stolen property. In the meanwhile, Barrett was living with a 14-year-old girl from Berea whom he had enticed with a mock marriage ceremony.

Sometime in the early 1930s, Barrett moved to Lockland, Ohio, though he continued to do business in Hamilton. Around 1935 he added car theft to his long and varied list of criminal acts. He stole a car in the middle of the night from the garage of a friendly couple of his acquaintance. Upon investigating, they discovered that Barrett had not only stolen the auto, but had also poisoned their watchdog.

Before long Barrett found an easier way to steal and sell cars. His method was to steal cars in various states, then take them to Hamilton where the autos would be altered and sold. He was wanted for grand theft auto in San Diego and St. Louis and was suspected of stealing cars in Kentucky, Tennessee and Ohio, as well. The fact that he crossed state lines with the hot cars made the crime a federal offense,

and the Federal Bureau of Investigation became very interested in Barrett and his activities. The FBI got a break in August 1935 when a man who lived in North College Hill purchased a stolen car from Barrett, who had carelessly signed the bill of sale.

Two years later, FBI Director J. Edgar Hoover wrote an article for the *American Magazine* in which he recalled the events leading up to Barrett's final murder.

The FBI planned to arrest Barrett for the interstate transportation of stolen vehicles. The word was that the suspect was about to leave town, so the authorities knew they had to move quickly. According to Hoover, the FBI agents telephoned Hamilton police, asking that they detain Barrett. Unfortunately, "Sitting in the police station was a man of supposed integrity who heard the officers talking about their plans to arrest Barrett. He informed Barrett that police and federal officers were looking for him." The wanted man took the hint and fled town. The eavesdropper's rash act would soon make him indirectly responsible for the loss of an agent's life.

Barrett headed for West College Corner, In., home of another brother named John. He was tracked down by two FBI agents, Donald McGovern and Nelson B. Klein. On the evening of August 16, around 6:15 p.m., the pair spotted Barrett and, after calling for backup, closed in and ordered him to surrender.

Barrett scrambled behind a garage, then hid behind a tree. He was not about to give up without a fight. Just as he had years before as a teenager facing down revenuers, the killer from the hills engaged his pursuers in a gun battle. He missed McGovern, but hit Agent Klein six times in the chest and arms with a .45 caliber revolver. In an incredible display of marksmanship, the mortally wounded Klein shot Barrett in the only exposed part of his body, his knee. The two agents shot Barrett in both legs, crippling the criminal for the rest of his life. Barrett would later claim, not too convincingly, that he opened fire because he thought the two men were feudists from Clay County come to extract vengeance.

Klein, a 37-year-old agent from Cincinnati, was killed in the line of duty. He left behind a widow and three children. As it turned out, shooting Klein was the gravest mistake Barrett could possibly have made. Congress had recently passed an act making it a mandatory capital offense to kill an FBI agent, and Barrett was among the first to violate the new law.

Barrett was taken to Fort Hamilton Hospital in Hamilton, Ohio, where he spent five days under heavy guard. Surgeons treated his injured legs and found they were beyond repair. Hoover claimed that Barrett boasted of the murder while in the hospital. He admitted the killing of his mother, but again feebly claimed it was in self defense. As the slayer recuperated, authorities tried to determine which state had jurisdiction over the case, as the town where the murder occurred was a mere 22 feet from the Indiana-Ohio border. It was established that the killing took place in Indiana, and Barrett was jailed in Indianapolis when he was released from the hospital on August 21.

The trial was held in December in an Indianapolis federal courtroom. Barrett, the cold-blooded killer with a glass eye and shattered legs, entered court in a wheelchair. (Hoover would later claim, rather absurdly, that Barrett was malingering in hopes of getting sympathy from the jury.) The *New York Times* remarked with ill-concealed amazement, "The quiet-spoken defendant [looks] more like a Main Street businessman than a mountaineer gunner." This was also noted by a reporter for the *Indianapolis Star,* who wrote that the killer's benign appearance made the biggest impression on spectators: "He didn't look the part" with his gray hair, neatly pressed gray suit, thick glasses, and his "half plaintive, high, soft voice."

Barrett was remarkably calm, sitting in his wheelchair with an omnipresent toothpick in his hand. His lawyer was Edward Everett Rice, an old friend and fellow Kentuckian. The defense attorney did what he could, but Barrett's guilt could hardly have been more obvious. In a desperate attempt to rehabilitate the defendant's image, Rice in his closing statement compared Barrett to Jesus Christ and urged the jury not to "crucify" his client. Spectators were more shocked than convinced by the poor analogy. One can only wonder what Klein's widow and three children, who attended each session of the trial, thought about it.

A few years earlier in Jackson County, Barrett was able to bribe his way to freedom after murdering his mother and sister, a circumstance recalled by District Attorney Val Nolan, who announced during his closing statement: "No Kentucky cousin of yours is trying *this* case, George Barrett!" On December 7, the jury deliberated less than an hour before finding him guilty. U.S. District Judge Robert C. Baltzell sentenced Barrett to be hanged the following March 23. The judge added, "May I add personally that I hope and pray that God will be merciful unto you."

Barrett quietly replied, "I think He will, your honor."

Hoover was pleased with the trial's outcome. He sent a telegram to the district attorney who prosecuted Barrett stating "I think the verdict marks a milepost on the roadway to proper law enforcement in this country."

As the day of the inevitable drew closer, Barrett expressed a wish to see his family. A telegram was sent by prison officials to one of Barrett's brothers, but he did not respond. To a group of relatives who did contact him, the convicted man warned, "Believe in God and obey the law and you'll never be in the position I'm in."

On March 19, the guards began keeping the prisoner under a constant death watch to prevent his committing suicide. Such precautions were not unwarranted. A couple of weeks previously, Barrett flew into a rage and threatened to take his own life in a bizarre manner: he would remove his glass eye, shatter it and swallow the broken shards. The guards took the optic away from him, and Barrett calmed down.

The day before the execution Barrett was visited by the state's official hangman, a farmer from Epworth, Ill., named Phil Hanna, who wanted to discuss the details of the hanging with Barrett, presumably to reassure the prisoner that his death would be painless. The two had a friendly conversation as Barrett enjoyed a meal of toast and coffee. "I have nothing against you," he said to his executioner. "What part do you do in this?"

"Well, I tie the noose and adjust it around his neck," replied Hanna.

"What do you mean?"

"I mean the rope."

"Oh yes, yes, the rope. I didn't understand you."

During the discussion, Barrett could clearly hear hammering

sounds as the gallows was being constructed outside. He remarked to a warden, "I'd five times rather die that way than be electrocuted." Shortly thereafter Barrett, a lifelong Baptist who had recently converted to Roman Catholicism, was given the last sacrament by the Reverend John McShane of St. Bridget's Catholic Church. The night before the sentence was to be carried out, Barrett called Sheriff Otto Ray for a last talk. The condemned man said, "I'll go out of this life with nothing to fear. I'm ready to die. I hold no malice toward anyone."

At eight o'clock on his final night on earth, Barrett ate his last meal with his sister Sylvania Woods, who had served jail time years before for aiding him when he lost his eye in a gunfight with authorities. After finishing the steak and fried potatoes, Barrett asked to see Father McShane and Dr. Robert Dwyer, prison physician. He also requested some reporters visit his cell for a final interview.

When the reporters entered his cell, Barrett took a glass eye from his pajama pocket— not the same one the guards had confiscated days earlier. "You see, boys, I have another glass eye. I have accepted the Catholic teaching that a suicide cannot enter Heaven. If I had had a table full of revolvers here in this cell, I would not have taken my life."

Then Barrett expansively told the press, "Boys, I called you here to tell you that I hold no malice toward anyone. I think everyone connected with this thing did his duty. I can't leave here hating anyone. I have nothing against you. When I leave here I know I've got a through ticket to Heaven. You can't go to Heaven hating anyone." Then he added, seemingly unaware of the thick irony of his statement, "I know I am going to Heaven and that I am going to meet my mother there."

Soon after his last words to the reporters, the execution took place on the night of March 23, 1936. It was the first hanging in Indianapolis in 50 years. The location was a tent in the north yard of the Marion County Jail. Barrett, holding a crucifix and clad in pajamas borrowed from Sheriff Ray, was carried to the scaffold on a stretcher borne by four lawmen. His eyes were steadfastly closed. As Barrett was carried to the gallows, Father McShane accompanied him, reading first from the Litany of Saints and then from the Book of Psalms. Because of Barrett's wounded legs, he had to be supported by deputies as the hood and noose were adjusted by hangman Hanna. The police closed an entire city block surrounding the prison to discourage throngs of morbid thrill seekers. (The jail had been inundated with nearly 1,000 letters from private citizens who wanted to see the execution. An estimated 80 percent of the requests were from women.) Nevertheless, there was no shortage of official eyewitnesses under the crowded tent as a heavy spring rain poured outside, including selected reporters, physicians, mortuary assistants and deputy marshals. An estimated 40 witnesses were gathered in all, among them two women.

Barrett stood on the trap door as if in a stupor. When asked whether he had any last words, the prisoner responded "No. Nothing." At 12:02 a.m., March 24, the trap was sprung by deputy sheriff Arthur Reeves just as Father McShane said "May God rest his soul." Barrett was officially pronounced dead 10 minutes later.

The morning of his execution, Barrett was buried in Holy Cross Cemetery in Indianapolis. The time of the funeral was kept secret to discourage crowds of onlookers. The gallows was quickly dismantled in the rain and shipped back to Murphysboro, Ill.

It is difficult to argue with *Time* magazine's assessment of Barrett's personality: "Few characters have come out of the Kentucky hills with a more impressive background for violence." But perhaps J. Edgar Hoover of the FBI, who encountered plenty of evil and violent criminals in his time, paid Barrett the ultimate testimonial. In 1937 Hoover flatly labeled George Barrett of Kentucky "The meanest man I ever knew."

Ben Wilson

Wanderer

One of Kentucky's finest eccentrics in recent times was Anderson County's Charles Ben Wilson, known as "Wandering Ben" due to his predilection for roaming far and wide in his bare feet. His habits and clothing made him picturesque enough to rate a cameo appearance in a Hollywood movie. Walking around without shoes may not seem a sufficient reason to achieve fame, but Wilson was not just an aimless wanderer. He was a homespun philosopher as well.

Wilson was born near Alton Station circa 1883. While a young man he developed an appreciation for two things: walking and horses, in particular show and harness horses. The former urge he indulged by walking to anyplace he felt like visiting. In 1907 he took a stroll to the northwestern United States and British Columbia, Canada. He supported himself by working as an irrigation engineer and did some logging in Washington. When he tired of that life in 1916, he walked back home to Anderson County, Ky., and made that his permanent residence whenever he wasn't struck by the whim to go roaming. He settled into life as an avid reader, wanderer and horseman on his 150-acre farm.

In some respects, Wilson's life is reminiscent of the 1994 film *Forrest Gump,* only that fictional character ran across the country while Wilson simply walked. Like Gump, Wilson and his lonesome sojourns captured the imagination of the media. *Courier-Journal* columnist Byron Crawford recalled that "Newspapers around the country carried pictures and stories of the barefoot, bearded old man, wearing only a pair of overalls rolled up to midcalf and walking with a long stick." One newspaper photo shows Wilson, looking for all the world like Santa Claus in overalls, standing barefoot in the snow. When the 1967 comedy *The Flim-Flam Man,* starring George C. Scott and Michael Sarrazin, was filmed on location in Anderson County, Wilson was invited to make a guest appearance. He stands out in a crowd scene that was shot outside the local courthouse. Wilson wears overalls, has a flowing white beard and carries a sign reading "Are you ready?" Later in the

"Wandering Ben" Wilson, walking barefoot through the snow on Lawrenceburg's College Street.

From the *Anderson News* of August 21, 1969. *Courtesy Anderson News.*

film, Wilson sits on a column in the courthouse lawn, watching impassively as a prisoner fights the police and escapes.

Like Forrest Gump, Wilson was prone to expressing nuggets of folksy philosophy that many found highly quotable. For example, in 1956 he observed, "This is the day of unlimited knowledge, but not unlimited wisdom. Our trouble is that our wisdom hasn't kept pace with our knowledge."

Also like Forrest Gump, Wilson was much wealthier than he appeared. He dressed and lived like a hobo simply because he wanted to. He once explained to a reporter that he did not wear shoes because they were uncomfortable, and preferred to "wear just enough [clothes] to be modest." He was such a shrewd judge of cattle and horses that he became a nationally noted authority on the animals and their pedigrees, and is mentioned as such in the 1951 edition of *Who's Who In Horsedom.* Rare was the county fair or horse show that Wilson did not attend, and breeders were quick to appreciate his insights and information. He was especially fond of the Kentucky State Fair and Lexington Junior League horse shows and camped out at the fairgrounds while the horse shows were in progress.

However, unlike the inoffensive and sweetly dimwitted fictional character Gump, Wilson could be sharp-tongued and sarcastic. Crawford mentions two incidents: Once someone asked Wilson what

people out West thought of his less-than-elegant clothing, only to receive the blunt answer "The people out West minded their own business." On another occasion when he was walking around Lawrenceburg in his bare feet on a bitterly frigid day, a well-intentioned soul inquired if his feet were cold. "Why, hell *yes* they're cold," was the uninviting response.

The legend of Wandering Ben was enhanced in 1950 when he journeyed to Louisville in order to sell his sister's cattle. The police saw the old barefoot man trudging down Fourth Street. They observed his long hair and matching beard and the overalls which had seen better days. They asked him where he was going. "It's none of your business who I am, where I'm going, or what I'm doing," he bantered.

Next thing Wilson knew, he was being arrested for loitering and disorderly conduct. But the roving eccentric had numerous friends among the state's cattlemen and horse breeders. They protested the arrest, and even complete strangers deluged the police with mail arguing that Wilson had the right to dress any way he wanted. Overwhelmed by the public's support for their oddly attired prisoner, officials dropped all charges and released Wilson. He received an apology, but Wilson got the last word when he told off the judge in elegant language that belied his appearance. He said, "I consider your treatment very ignorant, cowardly, and overbearing. I hold nothing but contempt for this court."

Though he did not suffer fools gladly, Wilson had an affection for children, often playing Santa Claus at Christmastime. He looked the part. When asked why he let his hair and beard grow so long, he replied "God put hair on my head for something, so I just let it be."

As late as 1964 Wilson was still hitching rides and walking to horse shows, but at last the time came when Ben Wilson could wander no more. He lived out his final years in a local nursing home called Sunset Hill. He died of pneumonia in a Lexington hospital on August 17, 1969, only about a month after some other men did some celebrated walking on the moon. He is still remembered by the citizens of Anderson County, and by citizens from several counties across the state, all because he loved to walk.

Offbeat Kentuckians

BIBLIOGRAPHY

"King" Solomon
Allen, James Lane. *Flute and Violin and Other Kentucky Tales.* New York: Harper and Brothers, 1891.
"Cholera." *Kentucky Gazette* 22 June 1833.
"Cholera." *Kentucky Gazette* 29 June 1833.
"Cholera." *Richmond* [Ky.] *Weekly Messenger* 28 May 1852.
Coleman, J. Winston. *Three Kentucky Artists.* Lexington: University Press of Kentucky, 1974.
Kolata, Gina. *Flu.* New York: Farrar, Straus, and Giroux, 1999.
"Monument to King Solomon Unveiled." *Lexington Herald* 19 Sep. 1908.
Thompson, Ronnie. "Man With A Royal Heart." *Lexington Herald-Leader* 10 Jan. 1960.
Wachs, Robert F. "Solomon, William." *Kentucky Encyclopedia.* Ed. John E. Kleber. Lexington: University Press of Kentucky, 1992.

Richard M. Johnson
"Col. R. M. Johnson." *Kentucky Gazette* 11 July 1839.
Devol, Edward. "Kentucky's Unsung Hero." *Courier-Journal Magazine* 19 Feb. 1978.
Felton, Bruce, and Mark Fowler. *Felton and Fowler's Famous Americans You Didn't Know Existed.* New York: Stein and Day, 1979.
"Johnson, Richard Mentor." *Encyclopedia of Kentucky.* New York: Somerset Publishers, 1987.
"Johnson, Richard Mentor." *Kentucky Encyclopedia.* Ed. John E. Kleber. Lexington: University Press of Kentucky, 1992.
Knobs. "Frankfort Correspondence." *Louisville Daily Journal* 9 Nov. 1850.
Meyer, Leland Winfield. *The Life and Times of Col. Richard M. Johnson of Kentucky.* New York: AMS Press, 1967. (Reprint of 1931 edition.)
Reed, Billy. *Famous Kentuckians.* Louisville: Data Courier, 1977.
Sifakis, Carl. *American Eccentrics.* New York: Facts On File, 1984.
Stimpson, George. *A Book About American Politics.* New York: Harper, 1952.

Jim Porter
Collins, Lewis. *History of Kentucky.* Revised by Richard Collins. Frankfort: Kentucky Historical Society, 1966. (Reprint of 1882 edition.)
"Death of James D. Porter, The 'Kentucky Giant.'" *Louisville Daily Courier* 26 Apr. 1859.
"Death of Jim Porter." *Louisville Daily Journal* 26 Apr. 1859.
Dickens, Charles. *American Notes.* Philadelphia: Bibliophilist Society, 1900.
Kendrick, William Carnes. *Reminiscences of Old Louisville.* N.p.: 1937.
"Kentucky Giant." *Scenic South* Mar. 1963.
"Large Funeral." *Louisville Daily Courier* 27 Apr. 1859.
"Largest Coffin Ever Made in Kentucky." *Louisville Daily Courier* 26 Apr. 1859.
"Porter, James D." *Kentucky Encyclopedia.* Ed. John E. Kleber. Lexington: University Press of Kentucky, 1992.
Reed, Billy. *Famous Kentuckians.* Louisville: Data Courier, 1977.
Webster, A. J. "Louisville in the Eighteen Fifties." *Filson Club History Quarterly* 4 (1930): 132-41.

Martin Van Buren Bates
Bates, Martin Van Buren. *The Kentucky River Giant.* n.d. (Reprinted by the *Hazard Herald.*)
"Bates, Martin Van Buren." *Kentucky Encyclopedia.* Ed. John E. Kleber. Lexington: University Press of Kentucky, 1992.
Drimmer, Frederick. *Very Special People.* New York: Bell, 1985.
Gould, George M., and Walter L. Pyle. *Anomalies and Curiosities of Medicine.* New York: Bell, 1956. (Reprint of 1896 edition.)
"Kentucky Giant Is Now A Farmer." *New York Times* 11 Mar. 1896.
Kunhardt, Philip B., Jr., Philip B. Kunhardt III, and Peter W. Kunhardt. *P. T. Barnum: America's Greatest Showman.* New York: Knopf, 1995.
Ratcliff, G. C. "Kentucky's Giant Awed the World." *Louisville Courier-Journal Magazine* 3 Nov. 1940.

John Banvard
Arrington, Joseph Earl. "John Banvard's Moving Panorama of the Mississippi, Missouri, and Ohio Rivers." *Filson Club History Quarterly* 32 (1958): 207-40.
"Banvard's Panorama of the Mississippi River." *Louisville Morning Courier* 1 July 1846.
"Death of a Unique Man." *New York Times* 19 May 1891.
Editorials. *Louisville Morning Courier* 30 June 1846.
Felton, Bruce, and Mark Fowler. *Felton and Fowler's Famous Americans You Didn't Know Existed.* New York: Stein and Day, 1979.
"The Great Three-Mile Painting To-Night!" *Louisville Morning Courier* 29 June 1846.
Guinness Book of Records. 1976 edition. New York: Bantam, 1976.
—— . 1996 edition. New York: Bantam, 1996.

Alexander McClung
Baldick, Robert. *The Duel.* London and New York: Spring Books, 1965.
Best, Edna Hunter. *Sketches of Washington, Mason County, Ky.* N.p.: 1936.
Chance, Joseph E. *Jefferson Davis's Mexican War Regiment.* Jackson and London: University Press of Mississippi, 1991.
Cochran, Hamilton. *Noted American Duels and Hostile Encounters.* Philadelphia and New York: Chilton Books, 1963.
Coleman, J. Winston. *Famous Kentucky Duels.* Lexington: Henry Clay Press, 1969.
Davis, Reuben. *Recollections of Mississippi and Mississippians.* Jackson: University and College Press of Mississippi, 1972.
Foote, Henry. *Casket of Reminiscences.* N.p.: Chronicle Publishing Co., 1874.
Kane, Harnett C. *Gentlemen, Swords, and Pistols.* New York: Bonanza, 1951.
McClung, Rev. William. *McClung Genealogy.* Pittsburgh: McClung Printing Co., 1904. (Reprinted 1983 by Print Shop, Dixon, Ill.)
A Mississippian. "Sketches Of Our Volunteer Officers: Alexander Keith McClung." *Southern Literary Messenger* Jan. 1855: 1-17.
Sands, Benjamin. *From Reefer to Rear Admiral: Reminiscences and Journal Jottings of Nearly a Half a Century of Naval Life.* New York: Frederick A. Stokes, 1899.
"Story Of a Brave Man." *New York Times* 27 Mar. 1855.

"Suicide." *Louisville Daily Democrat* 28 Mar. 1855.
"Suicide of A. K. McClung." *Louisville Daily Courier* 28 Mar. 1855.

Willis Westray
Craig, Berry. "The Man They Buried On His Feet." *Rural Kentuckian* Feb. 1986.
Graves County Genealogical Society. *Graves County, Ky., Cemeteries, Volume 4.* Mayfield, Ky.: Mayfield Printing Company, 1984.

Charles Bramble
Bramble Obituary. [Harrison County] *Log Cabin* 8 Jan. 1897.
"Buried In Whiskey." *Louisville Courier-Journal* 4 Jan. 1897.
"Floating in Finest Whisky." *Louisville Times* 4 Jan. 1897.
"Kentucky News: Stone Coffin." *Richmond Climax* 6 Jan. 1897.
"Rosewood Casket." *Lexington Morning Herald* 6 Jan. 1897.

Laura Irvin
Eastman, Mary, and Mary Bolté. *Dark and Bloodied Ground.* Riverside, CT.: Chatham Press, 1973.

Tom and Leo Mitchell
"Coins, Cigarettes, Comb, Mirror Placed in Double Grave of Gypsy Brothers." *Lexington Herald* 16 Apr. 1935.
Crawford, Byron. "Gypsy Death Rituals Go On Long After Burial." *Louisville Courier- Journal* 18 Jan. 1985.
"Funeral Held For Gypsy Dead Held Today." *Richmond Daily Register* 15 Apr. 1935.
Miller, James A., Jr. "One Killed As Truck Hits Gypsy Caravan." *Richmond Daily Register* 12 Apr. 1935.
"Mitchell Is Near Death." *Richmond Daily Register* 13 Apr. 1935.
"Second Gypsy Dies in Madison Crash." *Louisville Courier-Journal* 14 Apr. 1935.
"Silver Coins, Cigarettes, Soap, Comb, Mirror Put in Coffin With Gypsy Pair Buried Here." *Richmond Register* 16 Apr. 1935.
"Truck Crashes Into Gypsy Caravan; One Dead." *Lexington Herald* 12 Apr. 1935.

Leonard "Live-Forever" Jones
Collins, Lewis. *History of Kentucky.* Revised by Richard Collins. Frankfort: Kentucky Historical Society, 1966. (Reprint of 1882 edition.)
"Death of Leonard Jones." *Louisville Daily Democrat* 31 Aug. 1868.
Kendrick, William Carnes. *Reminiscences of Old Louisville.* N.p.: 1937.
"Live-Forever Jones." *Louisville Daily Courier* 12 Sep. 1868.
"Victim of an Idea." *Louisville Daily Courier* 1 Sep. 1868.

Simon Kracht
Adams, Jim. "Digging Up the History of U of L's 'Resurrector.'" *Louisville Courier-Journal* 2 Feb. 1992.
"Funeral of Simon Kracht." *Louisville Courier-Journal* 15 Nov. 1875.
"A Janitor's Life and Death." *Louisville Ledger.* Reprinted in *Pittsburgh Evening Leader* 24 Nov. 1875.
"Twenty Grains of Morphine." *Louisville Courier-Journal* 13 Nov. 1875.

Phil Arnold
Bishop, Jim. "Elizabethtown Man Made It Big With a Bag of Diamonds." *Elizabethtown News-Enterprise* 14 Mar. 1978.
Ferguson, Henry N. "Double Deal At Diamond Mesa." *American History Illustrated* Spring 1982.
Kinsner, Sandy. "Ghost Story." *Elizabethtown News-Enterprise* 26-28 Oct. 1984.
Liebling, A. J. "Annals of Crime: The American Golconda." *New Yorker* 16 Nov. 1940.
Mehling, Harold. *Scandalous Scamps.* New York: Ace, 1956.
Woodard, Bruce A. *Diamonds In the Salt.* Boulder, Co.: Pruett Press, 1967.

"Honest Dick" Tate
"Believed To Be Dead." *New York Times* 9 Aug. 1890.
Biographical Encyclopaedia of Kentucky of the Living and Dead Men of the Nineteenth Century. Cincinnati: J. M. Armstrong, 1878.
"Defaulted!" *Louisville Courier-Journal* 21 Mar. 1888.
"Early Defalcations." *Louisville Courier-Journal* 24 Mar. 1888.
"Impeached." *Louisville Courier-Journal* 31 Mar. 1888.
Klotter, James C. *History Mysteries.* Lexington: University Press of Kentucky, 1989.
——— . "Tate, James W." *Kentucky Encyclopedia.* Ed. John E. Kleber. Lexington: University Press of Kentucky, 1992.
Mittlebeeler, Emmet V. "The Great Kentucky Abscondion." *Filson Club History Quarterly* (27) 1953: 335-52.
"The State Treasurer." Editorial. *Louisville Courier-Journal* 21 Mar. 1888.
Tapp, Hambleton, and James C. Klotter. *Kentucky: Decades of Discord, 1865-1900.* Frankfort: Kentucky Historical Society, 1977.
"To Be Sifted." *Louisville Courier-Journal* 23 Mar. 1888.
"$250,000!" *Louisville Courier-Journal* 22 Mar. 1888.

Joseph Mulhattan
Edwards, Frank. *Stranger Than Science.* New York: Lyle Stuart, 1959.
Herringshaw, Thomas W. *Biographical Review of Prominent Men and Women of the Day.* Chicago.: A. B. Gehman and Co., 1888.
"The Liar A Thief Also." *New York Times* 12 Nov. 1891.
MacDougall, Curtis. *Hoaxes.* New York: Macmillan, 1940.
"A Modern St. Patrick." *Louisville Courier-Journal* 23 Mar. 1888.
Nickell, Joe. *Secrets of the Supernatural.* Buffalo, NY: Prometheus, 1988.
"Pat's Profit." *Richmond Climax* 4 Apr. 1888.
Pittsburgh Leader. Untitled story. 23 Oct. 1904.
" 'Prince of Liars' Fined." *New York Times* 13 Dec. 1902.
"Snake Bit." *Richmond Climax* 7 Mar. 1888.

Offbeat Kentuckians

Henry Wooldridge

Graves County Genealogical Society. *Graves County, Ky., Cemeteries, Volume 5.* Mayfield, Ky.: Mayfield Printing Company, 1985.
"Wooldridge Monuments." *Kentucky Encyclopedia.* Ed. John E. Kleber. Lexington: University Press of Kentucky, 1992.
Yates, Col. Nathan. *The World Famous Wooldridge Monuments.* Pamphlet. Mayfield, Ky.: Mayfield Printing Co., n.d.

William Goebel

Burdette, Dick. "Museum Marks Goebel's Murder." *Lexington Herald-Leader* 31 Jan. 2000.
"Goebel Is Shot By An Assassin." *New York Times* 31 Jan. 1900.
"Goebel Killed For $1,600." *New York Times* 7 Apr. 1900.
Harrison, Lowell H. "Goebel, William." *Kentucky Encyclopedia.* Ed. John E. Kleber. Lexington: University Press of Kentucky, 1992.
"In The Philippines When Goebel Was Shot." *Louisville Courier-Journal* 24 Sep. 1907.
"Kentucky Suspect Held." *New York Times* 7 Mar. 1900.
Klotter, James C. "Goebel Assassination." *Kentucky Encyclopedia.* Ed. John E. Kleber. Lexington: University Press of Kentucky, 1992.
— . *History Mysteries.* Lexington: University Press of Kentucky, 1989.
— . *William Goebel: The Politics of Wrath.* Lexington: University Press of Kentucky, 1977.
— . "William Sylvester Taylor" and "William Goebel." In *Kentucky's Governors 1792-1985.* Ed. Lowell H. Harrison. Lexington: University
    Press of Kentucky, 1985.
"Laying Crime On Dead Man." *Louisville Courier-Journal* 22 Sep. 1907.
Pearce, John Ed. *Days of Darkness: The Feuds of Eastern Kentucky.* Lexington: University Press of Kentucky, 1994.
Renneisen, Richard. "The Last Word On Goebel's Deathbed." *Louisville Courier-Journal* Magazine 21 May 1939.
Woodson, Urey. *The First New Dealer.* Louisville: Standard Press, 1939.

Carry Nation

Asbury, Herbert. *Carry Nation: The Woman With the Hatchet.* New York: Knopf, 1929.
"Bullets Fly Under Carrie Nation's Feet." *San Francisco Examiner* 13 Oct. 1904.
"Carrie Nation Arrested." *New York Times* 7 Apr. 1902.
"Carrie Nation Badly Hurt." *New York Times* 23 July 1904.
"Carrie Nation's Tirade at the Horse Show." *New York Times* 21 Nov. 1902.
"Glasgow Mobs Mrs. Nation." *New York Times* 15 Dec. 1908.
"Mob Threatens Mrs. Nation." *New York Times* 27 Jan. 1901.
"Mrs. Nation Annoys Senate." *New York Times* 20 Nov. 1903.
"Mrs. Nation Arrested." *New York Times* 5 Feb.1902.
"Mrs. Nation At Work Again." *New York Times* 24 Jan. 1901.
"Mrs. Nation Begins Her Crusade Anew." *New York Times* 22 Jan. 1901.
"Mrs. Nation Horsewhipped." *New York Times* 25 Jan. 1901.
"Mrs. Nation Smashes Bottles Galore." *New York Times* 15 Dec. 1903.
Reed, Billy. *Famous Kentuckians.* Louisville: Data Courier, 1977.
Smith-Peters, Lise. "Nation, Carry Amelia (Moore)." *Kentucky Encyclopedia.* Ed. John E. Kleber. Lexington: University Press of Kentucky, 1992.
"Stoned Her Audience." *New York Times* 20 Aug. 1905.
Strange Stories, Amazing Facts of America's Past. Ed. Jim Dwyer. Pleasantville, NY: Reader's Digest Association, 1989.
Taylor, Robert Lewis. *Vessel Of Wrath: The Life and Times of Carry Nation.* New York:
    New American Library, 1966.

William Van Dalsen

"Again Van Dalsen Takes Pencil in Hand to Explain." *Louisville Courier-Journal* 23 Sep. 1904.
"Bloody Deed." *Louisville Courier-Journal* 20 Sep. 1904.
"Confesses in Horrible Detail Murder of Fannie Porter." *Louisville Courier-Journal* 21 Sep. 1904.
"Confession of a Fiend." *Lexington Herald* 22 Sep. 1904.
"Extreme Penalty of the Law Given Van Dalsen." *Louisville Courier-Journal* 22 Nov. 1904.
"Grewsome Device." *Los Angeles Times* 26 Dec. 1904.
"In Effigy William Van Dalsen Hangs Himself." *Louisville Courier-Journal* 26 Dec. 1905.
"Murderer Has Been Found. " *Lexington Herald* 21 Sep. 1904.
"No Bond." *Louisville Courier-Journal* 24 Sep. 1904.
"Noose For Slayer of Fanny Porter." *Louisville Times* 22 Nov. 1904.
"Pays Penalty On Scaffold." *Louisville Courier-Journal* 20 Jan. 1906.
"Refuses Kiss." *Louisville Courier-Journal* 19 Jan. 1906.
"Tires of Lying in Jail." *Louisville Times* 21 Oct. 1904.
"Van Dalsen Met Death Gamely." *Lexington Herald* 20 Jan. 1906.
"Van Dalsen Must Die." *Louisville Courier-Journal* 19 Jan. 1906.
"Van Dalsen's Death May Be Delayed By Legal Technicalities." *Louisville Courier-Journal* 7 Jan. 1906.
"Young Woman Murdered." *Lexington Herald* 20 Sep. 1904.

Nathan Stubblefield

Breed, Allen G. "Irate Pop Singer Seeks Recognition For Grandfather As Radio's Inventor." *Lexington Herald-Leader* 25 May 1991.
Edwards, Frank. *Stranger Than Science.* New York: Lyle Stuart, 1959.
"Inventor Gives A Public Test of the Wireless Telephones." *Louisville Courier-Journal* 3 Jan. 1902.
"A Kentuckian Invents A Wireless Telephone System." *Louisville Courier-Journal* 26 Dec.1901.
"Kentucky Farmer Invents Wireless Telephone." *St. Louis Post-Dispatch* 12 Jan. 1902.
Mofield, William Ray. "Stubblefield, Nathan Beverly." *Kentucky Encyclopedia.* Ed. John E. Kleber. Lexington: University Press of Kentucky,
    1992.
"Radio Pioneer Dies, Poor and Embittered." *New York Times* 24 Apr. 1928.
Strange Stories, Amazing Facts of America's Past. Ed. Jim Dwyer. Pleasantville, NY: Reader's Digest Association, 1989.

John Shell

Brewer, Mary T. *Rugged Trail to Appalachia.* Viper, Ky.: Graphic Arts Press, 1978.
Cunagin, Judy Murray. *1880 Leslie County Kentucky Census.* Indianapolis: n.p., c1992.
Greene, James S., III. "Shell, John." *Kentucky Encyclopedia.* Ed. John E. Kleber. Lexington: University Press of Kentucky, 1992.
"His Years Highly Exaggerated." Editorial. *New York Times* 12 July 1922.
"John Shell Dies at Age of 134." *Louisville Courier-Journal* 10 July 1922.
"John Shell, 'Oldest Man in the World,' Dead at Home in Leslie County." *Lexington Herald* 10 July 1922.
"'Oldest Man in World' is Buried in Kentucky." *New York Times* 11 July 1922.
"Passing Of A Patriarch." Editorial. *Lexington Herald* 11 July 1922.
"Says 133d Birthday Makes Him the Oldest Living Person." *New York Times* 12 Sep. 1921.
Sizemore, Darlene. *1900 Leslie County Kentucky Census.* Dayton, Oh.: n.p., 1992.
Stidham, Sadie Wells. *Pioneer Families of Leslie County.* Berea: Kentucke Imprints, 1986.
"Uncle Johnny." Editorial. *Louisville Courier-Journal* 11 July 1922.
Welch, James E., Sr. *Clay County 1850.* Oneida, Ky.: Mountaineer Press, Oneida Baptist Institute, 1984.
Wilson, Jess D. *When They Hanged The Fiddler.* Berea: Kentucke Imprints, 1978.

Edgar Cayce

Carroll, Robert Todd. "The Skeptic's Dictionary." Online website. 1998. http://www.skepdic.com
Edgar Cayce Reader. Ed. Hugh Lynn Cayce. New York: Warner Books, 1969.
Edwards, Frank. *Strange People.* New York: Lyle Stuart, 1961.
"Illiterate Man Becomes A Doctor When Hypnotized." *New York Times* 9 Oct. 1910.
Randi, James. *Flim-Flam!* New York: Prometheus, 1987.
Smith, Warren. *Strange Powers of the Mind.* New York: Ace Books, 1968.
Stearn, Jess. *Edgar Cayce— The Sleeping Prophet.* New York: Doubleday, 1967.
Sugrue, Thomas. *There Is A River: The Story of Edgar Cayce.* New York: Holt, Rinehart, and Winston, 1942.

Death Valley Scotty

America's Castles. A&E Network. 1996.
"Chicago Mob Scares Death Valley Croesus." *New York Times* 12 July 1905.
Coolidge, Dane. *Death Valley Prospectors.* New York: Dutton, 1937.
Crawford, Byron. *Kentucky Stories.* Paducah: Turner Publishing Co., 1994.
"Death Valley Scott is Sued by His Wife." *New York Times* 18 Jan. 1937.
"Death Valley Scott Sheds 25-Year Pose." *New York Times* 8 Feb. 1930.
"Death Valley Scotty Asserts He Is Broke." *New York Times* 15 Jan. 1937.
"Death Valley Scotty Back To Buy Some More Mules." *New York Times* 10 Mar. 1936.
"Death Valley Scotty Is Dead at Age of 81." *New York Times* 6 Jan. 1954.
"Desert Scotty's Rites." *New York Times* 8 Jan. 1954.
Ernst, John. "Scott, Walter E." *Kentucky Encyclopedia.* Ed. John E. Kleber. Lexington: University Press of Kentucky, 1992.
Federal Writers' Project of the Works Progress Administration of Northern California. *Death Valley: A Guide.* Boston: Houghton Mifflin, 1939.
Kirk, Ruth. *Exploring Death Valley.* Stanford: Stanford University Press, 1965.
"Miner Starts Costly Trip." *New York Times* 10 July 1905.
"A Mystery From the Wild West." Editorial. *New York Times* 17 July 1905.
"Rush For Scotty's Mine." *New York Times* 29 Aug. 1905.
"Scott Starts For New York." *New York Times* 14 July 1905.
"Scott the Miner a Man of Legend." *New York Times* 9 Feb. 1930.
"Scotty, 'Broke' Week Ago, Offers $10,000 Bill at Bar." *New York Times* 25 Jan. 1937.
"Scotty Disdains Waldorf." *New York Times* 26 July 1905.
"Scotty Has $100,000 Buried in Mountains." *New York Times* 14 Mar. 1940.
"Scotty is Called 'Cheat.'" *New York Times* 15 Mar. 1941.
"Scotty is 61 Today." *New York Times* 20 Sep. 1936.
"Scotty Renounces Death Valley Mine." *New York Times* 14 Mar. 1941.
"Scotty Shot, But Not Much Hurt." *New York Times* 27 Dec. 1905.
"Scotty's Castle Exempt." *New York Times* 12 June 1941.
"Scotty's' Mine." Editorial. *New York Times* 8 Sep. 1905.
"Sue Death Valley Scotty." *New York Times* 1 Aug. 1940.
"Think 'Scotty' Murdered." *New York Times* 21 Dec. 1905.
"Wins Desert Mine Claims." *New York Times* 15 July 1941.

Speedy Atkins

Bartleman, Bill. "Farewell To Speedy." *Paducah Sun* 6 Aug. 1994.
"Find Drowned Body of Negro in River." *Paducah Sun* 31 May 1928.
Fisher, Frank. "Goodbye To Speedy." *Lexington Herald-Leader* 6 Aug. 1994.
Robertson, John E. L. *Paducah: A Pictorial History.* St. Louis: G. Bradley Publishing, Inc., 1988.

Tod Browning

Brosnan, John. *The Horror People.* New York: Plume, 1976.
Clarens, Carlos. *An Illustrated History of the Horror Film.* New York: Capricorn, 1967.
DeBartolo, John. Review of *The Unknown.* The Silents Majority. Online website. 1998. www.mdle.com/ClassicFilms
House, Thomas M. "Browning, Charles Albert." *Kentucky Encyclopedia.* Ed. John E. Kleber. Lexington: University Press of Kentucky, 1992.
"Killer Haunted By Chaney." *New York Times* 11 Jan. 1929.
MacIntyre, Diane. "Tod Browning: The Wizard of Odd." The Silents Majority. Online website. 1997-8. www.mdle.com/ClassicFilms
"Mystery Film Director." *New York Times* 24 Nov. 1929.
Nash, Jay Robert and Stanley Ralph Ross. *Motion Picture Guide.* Chicago: Cinebooks, 1986.

Offbeat Kentuckians

Peary, Danny. *Guide for the Film Fanatic.* New York: Fireside Books, 1986.

Skal, David and Elias Savada. *Dark Carnival: The Secret World of Tod Browning, Hollywood's Master of the Macabre.* New York: Anchor/Doubleday, 1995.

George Barrett

"Aged Jackson County Widow Slain By Son." *Lexington Herald* 3 Sep. 1930.

"Barrett Carried to Scaffold, Executed In Borrowed Pajamas." *Louisville Courier-Journal* 24 Mar. 1936.

"Barrett Death Watch Starts." *Indianapolis Star* 20 Mar. 1936.

"Barrett Gives Up To Officials." *Berea Citizen* 30 Apr. 1931.

"Barrett Hangs For Slaying Of Federal Agent." *Indianapolis Star* 24 Mar. 1936.

"Barrett Ready For End; Given Final Services." *Indianapolis Star* 23 Mar. 1936.

Bostwick, Mary E. "Barrett Trial Fast Yet Most Austere." *Indianapolis Star* 22 Mar. 1936.

"Crippled Killer." *Time* 30 Dec. 1935.

"Federal Agent Is Slain." *New York Times* 17 Aug. 1935.

"First Slayer Doomed By New Federal Law." *New York Times* 8 Dec. 1935.

"George Barrett, Accused of Killing Mother, Surrenders." *Jackson County Sun* 30 Apr. 1931.

"George Barrett Dies On Scaffold; Is Carried To Gallows On Stretcher." *Lexington Herald* 24 Mar. 1936.

Hoover, J. Edgar, and Courtney Ryley Cooper. "The Meanest Man I Ever Knew." *American Magazine* Apr. 1937.

"Hung Jury in Barrett Case." *Jackson County Sun* 14 Jan. 1932.

"Kentucky Man Slays Mother." *Louisville Courier-Journal* 3 Sep. 1930.

"Killer Is Doomed In Federal Court." *New York Times* 15 Dec. 1935.

"Matricide Is Still At Large." *Louisville Courier-Journal* 4 Sep. 1930.

"Order Quick Trial In Agent's Killing." *New York Times* 18 Aug. 1935.

Pearce, John Ed. *Days of Darkness: The Feuds of Eastern Kentucky.* Lexington: University Press of Kentucky, 1994.

"Search For Slayer." *Lexington Herald* 4 Sep. 1930.

"Services Held For Barrett." *Indianapolis Star* 25 Mar. 1936.

"$700 Reward for George W. Barrett." *Jackson County Sun* 11 Sep. 1930.

"Son Kills Aged Mother." *Berea Citizen* 4 Sep. 1930.

"Son Murders His Mother and Wounds His Sister In Family Wrangle Tuesday." *Jackson County Sun* 4 Sep. 1930.

"State Offers Reward for Arrest of Barrett." *Jackson County Sun* 11 Sep. 1930.

"U.S. Agent Slain Near Ohio Border." *Indianapolis Star* 17 Aug. 1935.

"Work Started For Execution." *Indianapolis Star* 22 Mar. 1936.

Ben Wilson

"Bearded Ben Wilson, Long Known to Horse Show Fans, Dies at 85." *Lexington Herald* 19 Aug. 1969.

"Ben Wilson, 85, Succumbs Sunday, After Long Illness." *Anderson News* (Lawrenceburg, Ky.) 21 Aug. 1969.

"C. B. Wilson, Familiar Sight at Fair, Dies." *Louisville Courier-Journal* 20 Aug. 1969.

Crawford, Byron. "Roaming Ben Wilson May Be Gone, But He Isn't Forgotten." *Louisville Courier-Journal* 20 Sep. 1982.